YOUR KNOWLEDGE HAS VALUE

Inducements, which led to the "Brexit". The United Kingdom's ambivalent relationship with the European Union

Lawrence Wighton

Bibliographic information published by the German National Library:

The German National Library lists this publication in the National Bibliography; detailed bibliographic data are available on the Internet at http://dnb.dnb.de.

ISBN: 9783346797926
This book is also available as an ebook.

© GRIN Publishing GmbH
Nymphenburger Straße 86
80636 München

Print and binding: Books on Demand GmbH, Norderstedt, Germany
Printed on acid-free paper from responsible sources.

The present work has been carefully prepared. Nevertheless, authors and publishers do not incur liability for the correctness of information, notes, links and advice as well as any printing errors.

GRIN web shop: https://www.grin.com/document/1316751

The United Kingdom's ambivalent relationship with the European Union – a qualitative analysis of the inducements, which led to the "Brexit" referendum

Bachelorarbeit

im Bachelorstudiengang

Politikwissenschaft

Am Institut der Sozial- und Wirtschaftswissenschaften

der Otto-Friedrich-Universität Bamberg

Verfasser: Lawrence Wighton

Table of Contents

I. Introduction

On the 23rd June 2016, the United Kingdom (henceforth referred to as: UK) held a referendum regarding its future within the European Union (henceforth referred to as: EU), in which "(…) 34 million Britons voted in a non-binding referendum with 51.9% casting their ballot in favour of the UK, which had joined in 1973, leaving the EU" (Welfens 2016, p. 539). The result of this referendum was "(…) arguably the most important political event in Europe since the fall of the Berlin Wall" (Fabbrini 2017, p. 1), shaking the foundations of the 'European idea' to its core, and leaving many experts baffled. Evans and Menon emphasise this sentiment by stating that "the British people had rejected the advice of their political establishment, of experts both foreign and home-grown. They had confounded academics and commentators alike by rejecting the status quo and voting for change" (Evans and Menon 2017, p. ix). However, while the results of this 'Brexit' (a combination of the words 'British' and 'exit') were largely astounding and unexpected, why did the UK opt for a referendum on its membership in the EU in the first place? While the potential reasons behind the outcome of the referendum have been subject to substantial academic analysis, research regarding the reasons for the referendum is somewhat scarce.

It is plausible that a combination of multiple reasons resulted in the UK's referendum decision. One of those could be the UK's general perception of insecurity in the international system – due to newly emerging threats, such as terrorism or other states. This could have resulted in the UK believing it to be 'safer' outside the EU, possibly feeling the EU was not doing 'enough' to procure its safety. It also seems plausible that domestic societal- or institutional factors, also played a role. Therefore, this dissertation will focus its analysis on two major areas of interest: the structure and configuration of the international system (along with the possible resulting concerns regarding national security), and domestic factors with societal, political, and institutional constellations. Based on these areas, Kenneth Waltz's neorealism – focusing on state's security concerns, due to the structure of the international system – and Andrew Moravcsik's liberal theory of international relations – with the focus on the role of domestic societal- and institutional factors in state's foreign policy decisions – could offer theoretical explanations for the UK's decision to hold a referendum. As such, this paper attempts to find a satisfying answer to the following research question: To what extent can the theoretical implications of Kenneth Waltz's neorealism and Andrew Moravcsik's liberal theory explain the United Kingdom's decision to hold a referendum on its membership in the European Union? To answer this question, I begin by defining the essential key terms used in this paper and laying down the theoretical assumptions and implications of Waltz's neorealism and Moravcsik's liberal theory. From these theoretical foundations I will derive my hypotheses – providing the main thread for the analysis – at the end of each theoretical chapter. The subsequent chapter discusses the research design of this paper. In the analytical portion of this dissertation, I will first focus on applying the relevant theoretical implications of neorealism to examine the referendum decision. Subsequently, I will similarly apply the compatible elements of Andrew Moravcsik's liberal theory to conduct an analysis into the reasons behind the referendum decision from a liberal perspective. Finally, I will discuss the conclusions drawn from the analysis.

II. <u>Definition and Clarification of Key Terms</u>

Before discussing any theoretical or empirical implications, it is essential to define the most relevant terms and phrases used throughout this paper. The first crucial word is '*Brexit*' – an amalgamation of the words 'British' and 'exit', used to describe the UK's intention to leave the EU. Throughout the course of this paper, this word will be used to describe the UK's intention to leave the EU. Another term is '*referendum*' – defined as "the principle or practice of submitting to popular vote a measure passed on or proposed by a legislative body or by popular initiative" (Meriam Webster's Collegiate Dictionary 2020). When put in the context of EU legislation, there is a difference between an 'accession referendum' and a 'withdrawal referendum' (Mendez and Mendez 2017, p. 19). The first term describes the process of non-EU member states contemplating to join the EU (ibid.), while the second describes a referendum that "(...) can only be held by an EU Member State, or a territorial entity that belongs to an EU Member State" (ibid.). When using the word 'referendum', I refer to a 'withdrawal referendum'. Finally, the phrase 'referendum decision' will appear numerous times in this dissertation – this phrase only refers to the UK deciding to hold a referendum on its membership in the EU, not the actual results of the referendum, after the British public voted.

III. Theoretical Foundations

The fundamental pillars of the analysis of the referendum decision are theory of neorealism by Kenneth Waltz and Andrew Moravcsik's liberal theory. In this chapter I present and discuss the foundations and the implications of those two theories – splitting this chapter into two separate sections to deal with each respective theory. It should also be noted that I do not provide a full in-depth representation of either theory, instead focusing solely on the elements of each theory that are relevant for the empirical analysis.

1. The Theory of Kenneth Waltz's Neorealism in International Relations

In this section, I outline the theoretical assumptions and components of Kenneth Waltz's neorealism and conclude by establishing my hypotheses for the empirical analysis.

1.1. The Implications and Assumptions of Waltz's Theory

Kenneth Waltz's theoretical foundation of neorealism was based on two main goals. The first was to find an explanation as to why bipolar and highly militarised states experienced phases of high tension and conflict potential, but also extensive phases of convergence and stability – as seen during the cold war (cf. Schörnig 2010, pp. 66 – 67). Secondly, the theory attempts to find an answer as to why the United States' hegemonic position in the late 1970s was no longer a given, because of the re-emergence of a post-war Europe as an economic power (cf. ibid., p. 66). Waltz bases his theoretical approach on the structure of the international system – instead of human nature, as classic realists do – so it is often referred to as a systemic theory.

According to Waltz "(…) a system is composed of a structure and of interacting units (2010, p. 79) – with structure being omnipresent throughout the whole system (cf. Masala 2014, p. 55), consisting of the units within it and the way in which these are arranged. The term 'units', in Waltz's definition refers to the actors in the system, which are the states (cf. Schörnig 2010, p. 71). As these units interact with each other continuously they are 'interacting units'. While these units or actors exist within this structure, the actors cannot directly influence the structure (cf. Schörnig 2010, p. 73) – but the structure can influence the actors, causing them to act similarly in certain circumstances (cf. ibid.). Neorealism assumes states to be homogeneous actors (cf. ibid., p. 71) – meaning that their inner domestic structure, for instance their political systems, is irrelevant from a neorealist perspective. Waltz does acknowledge other units, such as nonstate actors (cf. 2010, p. 94) – but indicates they have little influence upon international politics (cf. Schörnig 2010, p. 72). The concept of 'structure' is highly abstract and cannot be observed as a physical construct. Thus, Waltz argues that the structure of the international system is a combination of three separate components, defining them as the (1) "ordering principle" (Waltz 2010, p. 88), (2) "character of the units" (ibid., p. 93) and the (3) "distribution of capabilities" (ibid., p. 97). With the research question in mind, I will focus on the first two components as they are the most relevant.

The first component, the 'ordering principle', refers to the way the units are arranged in the international system. Waltz distinguishes between two different possible arrangements: a *hierarchic* arrangement, and an *anarchic* arrangement (cf. Waltz, p. 114). The first implies the existence of a hierarchical structure in which a superior entity has the power to sanction and protect the units within its structure (cf. Schörnig 2010, p. 73) – as can be observed in in domestic politics (cf. Diez et al. 2011, p. 180). Conversely, '*anarchy*' implies the structure does not have a superior entity to sanction and protect the units within. Waltz characterises the international system as being an environment where "(…) none is entitled to command (…)" (2010, p. 88) and "(…) none is required to obey…" (ibid.). Thus, he believes the international system to be "(…) decentralised and anarchic" (ibid.) in the absence of a 'world government' (cf. Schörnig 2010, p. 73). This anarchic environment forces states to behave in certain ways. Thus, the concept of *anarchy* is a central aspect of neorealism used to explain states' behaviour in the international system.

As *anarchy* is the prominent condition under which states exist in the international system, the implication is that the system is characterised by a constant state of *insecurity* (cf. Waltz 2010, p. 102), meaning states can never be sure of the intentions of the other states since there is no higher entity that could offer protection from an attack (cf. Gu 2000, p. 48). Waltz believes 'self-help' to be the most effective strategy for states to protect themselves in the international system (cf. 2010, p. 92), as there is no one else to rely on or call for help. The concept of 'self-help' and its implication for states brings us to

Waltz's second structure component: the "(…) character of the units (…)" (Schörnig 2010, p. 73). Here Waltz focuses on the functional differentiation of the units (cf. ibid.) – where there is a "(…) division of labour (…)" (ibid.) among the states, i.e., individual states fulfil different functions (ibid.). According to Waltz however, the presence of anarchy in the international system results in states not conducting this functional differentiation, instead leading to states pursuing their own interests and making the 'survival' in the international system their main preference. He argues: "In an unorganised realm each unit's incentive is to put itself in a position to be able to take care of itself since no one else can be counted on to do so. The international imperative is "take care of yourself"!" (2010, p. 107). In maximising their own security at all costs, and enabling them to survive, the theory of neorealism posits that states are only 'safe', when there is a 'balance of power' within the international system. The 'balance of power theory' is a 'sub-theory', within neorealism that focuses on states' strategies to maximise their security and will be examined in the following chapter.

1.2. The 'Balance of Power' Theory Within Waltz's Neorealism

As argued previously, the conditions of anarchy lead to states having to resort to a strategy of 'self-help', prioritising maximal security (cf. ibid., p. 111). Neorealism suggests that the only way to achieve the maximum amount of security in the international system is to create a 'balance of power' in the system. This balance would deter aggressive states from attacking others as there is a chance they would be defeated (cf. Schörnig 2010, p. 74). Neorealism posits that states will do everything to avoid an imbalance of power in the international system – if one state becomes too powerful, it could threaten the other state's ability to maximise their security. Diez et al. point out that "once a state is confronted with an adversary who has become powerful enough to be perceived as a potential threat, Waltz argues it can only choose the option of balancing" (2011, p. 181). This strategy of 'balancing' can occur in two different ways. The first option is increasing national power through *internal balancing* (cf. Masala 2014, p. 74) – by increasing military armament, the strengthening of the national economy or the development of better strategies (cf. ibid.). The second strategic approach states can choose is *external balancing* – characterised by forming alliances with other states (cf. Masala 2014, p. 74).

Regardless of the strategy states choose, the fundamental objective is to remedy the "(…) skewed distribution of relative power in the international system" (Layne 1993, p. 12) The theory also assumes that, if a state utilises its power resources to advance its position in the international system it is unlikely that other states will attempt to unilaterally compete with it. However, many states do not possess the necessary resources for huge military armaments, as the most powerful do, and so need to combine their resources with other weaker states in the form of alliances to restore the balance in the system (cf. Schörnig 2010, pp. 75 – 76). Finally, it must be emphasised that every state is a "(…) sovereign political entity (…)" (Masala 2014, p. 55). According to Waltz, this does not imply, however, that every state can act in any manner it wants, as the original meaning of 'sovereign' would suggest, but rather that every state "(…) decides for itself how it will cope with its internal and external problems, including whether or not to seek assistance from others and in doing so to limit its freedom by making commitments to them" (2010, p. 96) acknowledging the fact that the structure of the system could potentially also lead to states employing strategies and coping-mechanism other than balancing (cf. ibid. 1997, p. 915).

1.3. The Hypotheses Derived from Kenneth Waltz's Neorealism

Based on the theoretical implications and assumption of Waltz's neorealism, relevant to this research question, I have derived three hypotheses. These will be used to analyse the inducements behind UK's decision to hold a referendum regarding its EU-membership: (1) The anarchic structure of the international system and the resulting insecurity for states in the international system leads to the UK's decision to hold a referendum on its EU-membership. (2) The pursuit of 'survival' in the international system and the maximisation of security are a driving force behind the UK's decision to schedule a referendum. (3) The necessity for self-help and strategic thinking in the international system, in the form of internal- and external 'balancing', plays a role in the UK's referendum decision.

2. Andrew Moravcsik's Liberal Theory of International Relations

In this chapter I provide a summarised overview of Moravcsik's new liberal theory – the theoretical structure of Moravcsik's framework and its implications – and conclude by establishing my hypotheses for the empirical analysis, derived from his theoretical approach.

2.1. Implications and Assumptions of Andrew Moravcsik's Liberal Theory

Andrew Moravcsik's liberal theory identifies a vital factor that can play an important role in explaining how states define their foreign policy: the domestic processes within states. While his theory primarily looks at collectively aggregated social interests and groups capable of acting, such as parties, unions, and religious groups, Moravcsik does acknowledge that every collective action being taken by a group can be ascribed to the actions of individuals (cf. Schieder 2010, p. 192). Considering that state preferences are influenced and formed by domestic societal groups and individuals and the assumption that these act rationally, Moravcsik postulates that states are 'rational unitary actors', implying that they act "(…) as a unitary and rational actor on behalf of its constituents" (Moravcsik 1998, p. 22). The term 'unitary' implies that, within international relations, states "(…) act "as if" with a single voice" (ibid.) – that is to say that state's positions and preferences are aggregated, formed, and brought onto one denominator, before entering the negotiation processes in international relations.

Moravcsik identifies the following three main assumptions to base his theoretical framework on: (1) The primacy of societal Actors, (2) representation of state preferences and (3) interdependence and the international system (cf. 1997, pp. 516 – 521). I will focus on the first two assumptions of the theory, as they are the most crucial theoretical components for the analysis – the last assumption will not be examined further, as it focuses on state interdependencies, which determine state's foreign policies (cf. Schieder 2010, p. 197). However, based on a preliminary analysis, these do not appear to be as relevant as potential domestic factors to explain the referendum decision.

2.1.1. The Role of Societal Actors

Moravcsik's first assumption in his liberal theory addresses the vital role of societal actors in international politics, as he believes that the actions, expectations and requirements of the individuals and societal groups have to be considered and evaluated – from an analytical perspective – before examining subsequent politics (cf. Moravcsik 1997, p. 517). When Moravcsik talks about societal actors, specifically, he is referring to 'individuals' and 'private groups' (cf. ibid., p. 516). Those individuals and groups "(…) define material and ideational goals independently of politics (…)" and "(…) then seek to advance those ends through political means" (Moravcsik 2010, p. 236). He postulates that these actors exhibit the following characteristics: They are "(…) on the average rational and risk averse and (…) organize exchange and collective action to promote differential interests and constraints imposed by material scarcity, conflicting values, and variations in societal influence" (Moravcsik 1997, p. 516).

Moravcsik states that the political process is ingrained into "(…) domestic and transnational society" (Moravcsik 1997, p. 517). He argues that the political process essentially finds its origins in the demands of an "(…) aggregation of boundedly rational individuals with differentiated tastes, social commitments, and resources (ibid.). He identifies globalisation as one of the main reasons for the diversity of the societal actors' societal interests (2010, p. 236), as engaging in "(…) transnational economic, social and cultural activity (…) changes the prospects for realizing domestic objectives" (ibid.). Moravcsik emphasises that the individuals in this societal mixture all form their own "material and ideational interests" (1997, p. 517), autonomously, outside of the political realm. Once these interests have been constructed, the societal individuals pursue them by attempting to implement them into the political discourse and process and through "collective action" (ibid.). Moravcsik presumes that "(…) political order and conflict result from the underlying pattern of such interactions" (2001, p. 5).

As mentioned above, Moravcsik believes the interests of societal actors to be diverse since they are influenced by a multitude of different factors. Consequently, the argument is made by Moravcsik that there is no such thing as "automatic harmony (…) among the individuals and groups in society" (1997, p. 517). Rather, there is a constant clash of diverging interests of the individuals and groups – where each individual or group continuously assesses their position and looks for opportunities to act to influence or shape the political process and aggregate those interest (cf. Moravcsik 1997, p. 517).

This clash of interests can create conflict between groups. Moravcsik identifies three factors, which he believes to be the elementary sources of conflict within a society: "divergent fundamental beliefs, conflict over scarce material good, and inequalities on political power" (ibid.). He elaborates by stating that "(…) irreconcilable differences in beliefs about the provision of public goods, such as borders, culture, fundamental political institutions, and local social practices, promote conflict" (ibid.). He also states that many social conflicts almost always end with there being 'winning' and 'losing' sides (cf. Moravcsik 2010, p. 237), meaning that one actor will most likely be achieving their preferential objectives. Additionally, Moravcsik posits that an unequal distribution of "societal influence" (Moravcsik 1997, p. 517) can be the source of conflicts. The reasoning behind this assumption is based on the premise that when equality in the distribution of social power is present the "(…) the costs and benefits of actions are more likely to be internalised to individuals" (ibid.). One way through this could be accomplished are "legitimate domestic political institutions" (ibid.). Conversely, when inequality in the social influence is present, some groups have the ability to circumvent the costs for the good redistribution and place this burden on the rest of society (ibid.; cf. Schieder 2010, p. 194).

Moravcsik's first assumption of his liberal theory emphasises the importance of societal actors, tracing a states' domestic and international behaviour and action back to the conflicts over interest between the societal actors. He underscores the fact that these societal factors must be examined and considered prior to assessing the political process, as it is heavily affected by them. Moravcsik argues that domestic and national politics are essentially the result of the conflicts being contested in society. Of course, this conflict does not take place in a 'law-less' environment. There are institutional as well as structural elements and restrictions, which affect the way the conflicts are 'fought out'. These are the central components of Moravcsik's second assumption in his liberal theory and will be discussed in the following chapter.

2.1.2. The Role of Institutions

Beyond societal actors, Moravcsik identifies two important factors that shape and determine the conflicts of interests: domestic institutions and the structures that are in place to act as interest mediators between society and the state (cf. Schieder 2010, p. 195). In his new liberal theory, Moravcsik sees states not as actors, but as "(…) a representative institution constantly subject to capture and recapture, construction and reconstruction by coalitions of social actors" (1997, p. 518). Institutions are therefore a representation of the societal preferences and the "(…) social power of individuals (…)" and the mechanisms by which these preferences are being converted into a state's foreign policy (ibid. 1997, p. 518; cf. Schieder 2010, p. 195). They are somewhat of a 'mirror-image' of society and its preferences. Logically, the policies that governments are trying to instigate are always influenced and constricted "(…) by the underlying identities, interests, and power of individuals and groups (inside and outside the state apparatus) who constantly pressure the central decision makers to pursue policies consistent with their preferences" (ibid. 1997, p. 518).

Of course, not all individuals and social groups receive the same amount of representation by governments, resulting in inequality in the level of influence they can have on structures and institutions (cf. ibid.), and factors such "(…) property, risk, information or organizational capabilities… may create social or economic monopolies able to dominate policy" (ibid.). Moravcsik also states that the specific characteristics of a representative institution play a major role in determining which societal groups can turn their own interests into national interests that are pursued by the state (cf. Schieder 2011, p. 195) – with many institutions 'catering' to specific societal interests. This implies that institutions are more likely to work in favour of some societal groups or individuals in pushing their interest and policies than for others. This leads to them, together with the societal interests as a separate element, being a fundamental factor that can explain a states behaviour in the international system (cf. Moravcsik 1997, p. 518).

Combining the first two core assumptions: states are not in constant pursuit to maximise their power and security – as domestic societal actors, which influence a state's foreign policy – and generally do not follow this 'security maximisation' approach. Instead, powerful domestic societal actors transmit their "(…) particular interpretations and combinations of security, welfare, and sovereignty (…)" (ibid., p. 519), influenced by institutions and structures, to the government, which formulates a foreign policy accordingly. These two basic assumptions of liberal theory will be central to the analysis of this paper.

2.2. The Hypotheses Derived from Andrew Moravcsik's Liberal Theory

From the theoretical assumptions and implications of Andrew Moravcsik's liberal theory, I have derived the following hypotheses which will be tested to conduct an analysis into the UK's decision to schedule a referendum on its EU-membership: (1) The interests and preferences of domestic societal actors and societal conflicts, play a significant part in the UK's decision to hold a referendum regarding its EU-membership. (2) Domestic institutions and structures play a role in the UK's decision to call for a referendum on its EU-membership.

IV. Research Design

The research design I employ in an attempt to answer the research question of this paper is a theory-driven case study, looking at the inducements behind the case of the referendum decision. This chapter will address the modus operandi for the subsequent analytical part of this case study.

Analysis Objective

The fundamental task of this paper is to answer the following research question: To what extent can the theoretical implications of Kenneth Waltz's neorealism and Andrew Moravcsik's liberal theory explain the United Kingdom's decision to hold a referendum on its membership in the European Union? To do so, I will analyse potential reasons that could have played a part in influencing the referendum decision to find if the selected theoretical frameworks can provide a plausible explanation for the UK's decision to hold a referendum.

Case Selection

The reason for analysing the inducements of the referendum decision find their foundations in the huge significance of the Brexit vote of 2016 and its implications for international relations. Although, as O'Rourke emphasises, "Britain's relationship with Europe
was always an ambivalent one" (2019, p. 175), the British public voting for the UK to
leave the EU still represented "(...) the biggest shock to the political establishment in
Britain and across Europe for decades (...)" (Asthana et al. 2016). This shows the relevance of this Brexit referendum, thus providing an impetus for the analysis behind the
fundamental reasons for the referendum decision.

Justification of the Theoretical Foundations

Considering the complexity behind the referendum decision and the fact that its subsequent result had a considerable impact on numerous aspects of international relations, it
makes sense to use a theoretical foundation, which offers a relatively wide array of assumptions and implications. Furthermore, the reasons behind the referendum decision
seem to be multi-facetted – with potentially both internal and external factors at work.
Waltz's neorealism – focusing on the structure and insecurity of the international system
along with the resulting strategic thinking of states – and Moravcsik's liberal theory –
which sees domestic societal factors as a determinant of foreign policy decisions – seem
to offer convincing theoretical constructs which can be used to analyse those factors. In
order to create a clear structure, each analysis will be conducted with each theory being
applied separately.

Justification of the Observational Period Employed for the Analysis

Analysing the entire period since the UK joined the EU up until the point it decided to
hold a referendum on its membership would go beyond the scope of this paper. Therefore,
the observational period relevant for the analysis of this paper is the period of time starting
on January 2013 and ending on February of 2016. The reason being: on the 23rd of January
2013, David Cameron – UK Prime Minister at the time – delivered a speech at the Bloomberg houses in London which explicitly announced, for the first time, that the UK would

hold a referendum on its EU-membership (cf. Evans and Menon 2017, p.9). The 'cut-off' point for my analysis is the 20th February 2016 – the day David Cameron officially announced, in a Downing Street speech, that the 23rd of June 2016 would be the day of the referendum on the UK's future in the EU (BBC 2016).

Method

The method applied to gain my empirical data and information from those sources, was an adapted version of Mayring's *qualitative content analysis* – as this particular method offers substantial ways to analyse and interpret different types of texts, which were the main sources for the analysis. Using this method, I hoped to find indications that point towards potential reasons the UK is adamant on leaving the EU. This analytical- and interpretational quality of the method further helped in the operationalisation process of the variables.

The objective of the qualitative content analysis is the examination of the actual meanings and implications of texts and documents and the connection of texts' contents with a theoretical foundation (cf. Mayring 2015, p. 13). Based on these implications, the method seemed appropriate to extract the relevant information needed to analyse the research question. For his content analysis model, Mayring identifies three different ways in which content analysis and interpretation can be conducted: explication, summary, and content structuring. While the first two methods were not applicable to the analysis in this paper, the latter, 'content structuring' was employed. The central purpose of the 'content structuring' technique is the filtering of the material to determine certain content, topics, and themes (cf. ibid., pp. 13 – 14). The type of contents, which are subject to extraction, have to be identified and classified through different categories, which are formed based on a theoretical foundation (cf. ibid.).

Considering that the analysis was based on text-based sources – and that it was interested in assessing the interests, preferences, and actions of actors, based on the content of these sources – this structured approach seemed the most logical to identify the relevant information. The 'creation' of the categories, used to extract relevant information, is strongly intertwined with the theoretical foundations, and aimed at finding an answer to the research question (cf. ibid., p. 13). However, in his method, Mayring does not construct the categories from potential research variables, derived from a theoretical approach (cf. Gläser and Laudel 2013, pp. 1 – 10). Nonetheless, in conducting my analysis, this seemed like a logical approach, as the analysis was based on theoretical foundations and attempted to test their implications and assumptions. Therefore, I adapted Mayring's method slightly, utilising Gläser and Laudel's method which suggests that the theoretical research variables can be used to structure and create an analytical framework to examine the sources (cf. ibid., p. 10). This means that the analytical categories were constructed from research variables which were constructed from the hypotheses. The categories used to extract the relevant data and information from these sources, were constructed deductively, meaning that I constructed and defined the categories prior to examining the material and extracting the data. After having constructed the categories, I examined the relevant material. Based on the key words and key concepts from these categories, I examined the sources in order to extract the relevant data and information. Upon locating relevant passages in the texts, providing valuable and insightful data, these were allocated to their specific category, according to their contents. The establishment of the 'extended category system', applied to identify the applicable data and information, and which helped to operationalise the research variables and specify the objects of investigation and the related categories, is elaborated on in the subsequent chapters.

Identification of Research Variables

Based on the derived hypotheses for each theory presented above and in order to create categories that will structure and specify the analysis, I identified the following research variables relevant for the analysis. By applying these variables to the dependent variable individually, I will examine how different factors may have influenced the referendum decision. Therefore, I am using the different relevant components and concepts of each theory applying them to the dependent variable to test their explanatory ability.

For the analysis from a **neorealist perspective:** The *independent variables* are the (1) anarchic structure and the insecurity of the international system and the (2) pursuit to 'survive' in the 'insecure' international system through 'self-help', in the form of internal- and external 'balancing', as a strategy to achieve this. The second variable combines the assumptions of the second and third hypotheses as this provides a more logical approach for the analysis. The *dependent variable* is the UK's decision to have a referendum on its EU-membership. For the analysis from a **liberal perspective**: The *independent variables* are the (1) interests and preferences of domestic social actors and (2) the domestic institutions and structures. The *dependent variable* is again the UK's decision to hold a referendum on its EU-membership.

Operationalisation

The analysis is split into two separate parts, each dealing with one of the theoretical approaches of this paper. In order to receive plausible results, I applied a qualitative content analysis, to assess the relevant text-based materials and sources for both respective analytical parts.

The first content analysis addresses the research question from a neorealist perspective. In order to test the dependent variables, which represent the categories structuring the analysis, from a **neorealist perspective**, I used the following empirical data and material in the qualitative content analysis:

The *first independent variable* addresses the *anarchic structure* of the international system and the resulting *insecurity* and thus the *perception of insecurity*, by states, in the international system. Therefore, I examined the UK's national security strategies since they represent an overall picture of the UK perceived international threats. Over the past decade, the UK has released two, potentially relevant, official national security strategies – in 2010 and 2015. Naturally, the 2015 strategy falls into the observational period of the paper and was therefore central to the analysis. However, I also included the 2010 security strategy to receive a more thorough picture of the UK's national security strategy over the past years. By examining the UK's defence strategies, I hoped to find evidence regarding the UK's perception of its security and the nature of potential threats in the international system and that it wants to leave the EU based on those threats.

Additionally, I looked at documents and papers by the UK's Ministry of Defence to find further evidence regarding the security and threat perception. In both, the strategies and the other documents, I tried to identify data indicating that the UK perceives the international system to be 'insecure' and that it perceived certain states or other international security issues as a threat to its national security and if this could be connected to the UK's referendum decision. Secondary sources were used to gain a more complete picture of the UK's perception of security in the international system.

The *second independent variable* of neorealism assesses *the 'desire' to survive in the international system through the means of 'self-help' and strategic thinking through internal- and external 'balancing'*. Suitable indicators that were used to examine these factors seemed to be military spending and the position of the UK regarding the pursuit of forming strategic alliances with other states or institutions. For the military spending indicator, I looked at the UK's military spending throughout the course of the observational period (2013 – 2016). Specifically, I attempted to find evidence which suggested that the UK prioritised procuring its own security through increased military investments rather than relying on other states, possibly indicating the intention to leave the EU. Potential indicators were the increase in national military spending, or decrease of monetary expenditures for defence institutions, such as NATO (North Atlantic Treaty Organization) or the EU defence institutions, such as the Common Security and Defence Policy (CSDP) and the Common Foreign and Security Policy (CFSP).

The '*strategic thinking through forms of internal- and external balancing*' variable was analysed in a similar manner. The military spending indicator was used to examine whether there was evidence suggesting that the UK had been strategically investing financial resources in military cooperation with other states to increase its security. Further, I again looked at the national security strategy to investigate whether the UK placed particular emphasis upon strategically cooperating with some certain states and institutions, but not with others, further potentially pointing towards the intention to leave the EU. When examining both variables, secondary sources were additionally considered to substantiate the potential evidence found in the primary sources.

In order to test the dependent variables, by applying the qualitative content analysis method, from a **liberal perspective**, I made use the following empirical data and material:

The *first independent variable* I will test, focuses on *the role of societal actors* in the formation of a foreign policy. First, it has to be established which specific societal actors I will be examining. The societal actors, who could have played a major role in the referendum decision were private- and other organised groups with aggregated preferences as well as individuals. This coincides with Moravcsik's conceptualisation of societal actors, which, among others, focuses on groups such as parties and unions (cf. Schieder 2010, p. 192). For the analysis I first focus on *interest groups*, within the UK, with economic incentives as well as socially relevant preferences, alongside individual actors within those groups. Secondly, I shifted the focal point to political actors. These will be addressed later on in this chapter.

The interest groups were picked according to their most significant economic and social relevance to the UK, since it is plausible that they would have been affected significantly, positively, or negatively, by a Brexit and therefore adopting strong positions regarding the subject. The interest groups with business and economic incentives relevant for the analysis were the Confederation of British Industry (CBI) and the trade Union 'Unite: the Union' (henceforth referred to as: Unite). The CBI was chosen because it is the UK's "(…) biggest lobby group (…)" (Groom and Parker 2014), representing the interests of 190.000 businesses, employing almost seven million people in the UK (cf. CBI 2020). Unite was the biggest trade union in the UK with economic preferences, during the observational period (cf. Morris 2013; cf. BBC 2014; cf. O'Connor and Pickard 2015).

In order to assess these groups' potential influence on the referendum decision, I examined position papers, newspaper articles and other publications, which indicate their respective positions and attitudes towards the referendum. Secondary literature was also used to further explore the interest group's positions. By examining those sources, I hoped to find statements which indicate intentions and preferences regarding the referendum decision. Moreover, I attempted to find evidence showing that the interest groups influenced politics in some way leading to the referendum decision.

Additionally, I placed the focus on *political actors* as further societal actors, with the most relevant being the Prime Minister, as an individual actor, and the Conservative Party and the UK Independence Party (UKIP) as collective actors. These actors were picked because it seems plausible that their strongly diverging preferences played a significant role in the referendum decision. Furthermore, The Conservatives were the governing party during most of the observational period and David Cameron Prime Minister (cf. BBC 2010; cf. BBC 2015d), suggesting their crucial role in the referendum decision. UKIP was chosen because of its long-standing 'anti-EU' stance (cf. Hunt 2014). In order to assess the individual positions of the Prime Minister, the most important sources were the transcripts of public speeches and statements. I examined those sources in an attempt to find indications regarding the Prime Minister forming his own preferences and interests and how this might have had an effect on the referendum decision. The positions of the other political actors were judged by analysing official government documents, papers as well as party manifestos. Again, I hoped to find evidence that shows those actors interests and their preferences and how they are trying to pursue them. In the examination of these variables, secondary sources will also support the evidence derived from the primary sources.

The *second independent variable* will test the role of *domestic institutions* and **structures** in the referendum decision. I analyse whether they possibly affected the preference formation of the societal actors and if they were potentially more beneficial to some actors than others in enabling them to pursue those preferences through the political process. The empirical material I considered were legal texts which primarily focus on the referendum. Significant legislative texts that could offer some valuable insights were the 2015 European Referendum Act and the 2014 Transparency of Lobbying, Non-Party Campaigning and Trade Union Administration Act.

V. <u>Empirical Analysis</u>

In the previous chapters of this paper, I have outlined and discussed the implications and assumptions of Waltz's neorealism and Andrew Moravcsik's liberal theory. These theories provide a coherent analytical construct which I will apply to conduct the analysis into the fundamental question of this paper – to what extent can these theoretical approaches deliver valuable insight into why the UK chose to hold a referendum on its EU-membership? As with the presentation of the theories, the analysis is separated into two sections, the first analysing the hypotheses from a neorealist perspective and the second section analysing the liberal hypotheses.

1. How can the United Kingdom's Referendum Decision be Explained?

In this chapter I will now conduct the analysis of the inducements behind the UK's refer-endum decision from the perspective of Waltz's neorealism and Moravcsik's liberal the-ory of international relations.

1.1. Analysis from a Neorealist Perspective

It seems plausible that the UK's decision to hold a referendum on its EU-membership was influenced by multiple different factors. One of these factors could be the foreign policy implications and certain constellations in the international system. These potential factors will be analysed in the following chapters applying the theoretical implications of Waltz's neorealism. First, I place the focus on the anarchic nature of the international system, before subsequently applying the 'survival' and 'self-help through strategic thinking' concepts of Waltz's theory to analyse the probable reasons for the referendum decision.

1.1.1. The Anarchic International System as a Relevant Factor

In his theory of neorealism, Waltz's implies the existence of an anarchic structure in the international system, creating a level of insecurity and causing states to act in certain ways (cf. Schörnig 2010, p. 73). This would suggest that the UK's perception of the insecurity in the international system, caused by anarchy, played a significant role in the referendum decision in some way. The subsequent analysis will attempt to find evidence that could indicate that the UK wanted to leave the EU due to the threats of an anarchic system, examining the national defence strategies of 2010 and 2015 as they present a "whole government" approach (The National Security Strategy 2010, p. 10).

Analysis of The United Kingdom's 2010 National Security Strategy

According to the 2010 strategy, one of the UK's main objectives was the preservation of national security (cf. ibid., 9). In order to attain this important objective, the 2010 strategy states that the UK will employ all of its "(…) national capabilities to build Britain's prosperity (…)", increasing its "(…) influence in the world and strengthen our security" (ibid.) and use its power to "(…) help shape a stable word" (ibid., p. 10). This coincides with the neorealist assumption that states want to pursue maximum security in the international system, acknowledging the anarchic and insecure structure. However, this does not imply any intentions of the UK wanting to hold a referendum on its EU-membership. In fact, the strategy states the "(…) vital partnership in the European Union" (ibid., p.10), is a key component to achieving this objective. The UK does also mention that it wants those institutions, it has alliances with, to reform in order to continue working effectively with them (cf. ibid.), which could point to the fact that the UK was unhappy with the state of the EU, as one of its alliances, at that point, since it was not providing effective support against insecurity of the anarchic international system.

The 2010 security strategy points out that the largest source of security threats "(…) arise from actions by others: States or non-state actors, who are hostile (…)" (ibid., p. 25) to the national interest of the UK. The main first tier threat perceived by the UK was international terrorism, especially from the terrorist organisation Al Qaeda (cf. ibid., p. 13). As another threatening factor, the strategy identifies the stability of some states in the international system (cf. ibid., p. 28), emphasising that "fragile, failing and failed states around the world provided the environment for terrorists to operate as they look to exploit ungoverned or ill-governed space" (ibid., p. 28). This points to the anarchy of the international system, which leads to states failing as they have to take care of themselves and creating an environment that is characterised by potential threats – in this case the growth of terrorism. The UK acknowledges and perceives this threat. The UK identifying terrorism as the main threat to its security suggests that they don't necessarily perceive other states to be the only probable source of attacks. This of course, contradicts the neorealist assumptions of other states usually being the aggressors. However, perhaps when considering the stability in Europe since the Second World War, a conjectural assumption could be made that, especially in Europe, states are not the main source of security threats anymore – they have been 'replaced' by international terrorism. Thus, it could be argued that terrorism can be associated with the neorealist perception of threats in the international system, due to anarchy. However, the 2010 security strategy does not specifically mention whether the EU takes on a central role on the UK's combat against international terrorism.

It simply states that the UK aims to "protect operational counter terrorist capabilities in intelligence and policing, and the necessary technologies to support them (…)" (ibid., p. 34.). Therefore, the strategy provides no clear indications that the threat of international terrorism to the UK was a driving factor behind the referendum decision.

When looking at the second tier of perceived threats, the UK considered "(…) an attack on the UK or its Overseas Territories by another state (…) using chemical, biological, radiological or nuclear (CBRN) weapons" to be a potential threat. However, it also states that the probability of this happening is relatively low, despite the significant impact (cf. ibid., p. 27). In the same vein, the strategy emphasises that the UK needs to "(…) prevent nuclear proliferation of the middle east" (ibid., p. 14). According to the strategy, Iran could pose a major threat if it were to acquire nuclear weapons (ibid., p. 14). Should this happen, it is feared that other states in close proximity would also pursue the 'acquisition' and development of nuclear weapons, which would have a severely destabilising effect on the respective regions (cf. ibid.). It is also feared that certain levels of instability could open up opportunities for terrorists to "(…) threaten the UK" (ibid., p. 27). This notion is confirmed by Hill, who accentuates that it has "(…) been immensely useful for Britain to work with fellow European states, in a variety of fora, in the pursuit of its concerns over Iran" (2019, p. 72). The 'nuclear threat' and the possibility of states using nuclear weapons to attack other states, is of course one that falls into the theoretical concept of anarchy and the framework of neorealism.

The anarchy, and the resulting lack of a higher entity which offers complete protection from such a threat, results in the UK identifying the 'nuclear threat' as one of the most potent threats, implying a feeling of 'insecurity' by the UK. However, the actions against the nuclear proliferation of states, especially Iran, required the UK to work closely together with other European states. Therefore, a referendum on its EU-membership would seem somewhat illogical. The strategy affirms this by stating that the UK needs to strengthen its "(…) network of bilateral ties with partners as well as traditional allies (…)" (National Security Strategy 2010, p. 15). Again, there is no indication that the UK intends to pursue a referendum on its EU-membership due to the potential insecurity of the international system.

The strategy also states that the UK currently faces "(…) no major state military threat" (ibid.) and places potential "(…) large scale conventional military attacks on the UK by another state (…)" (ibid., p. 27) in the third tier of threats, highlighting the low likelihood. While the UK is not expecting military attacks, it does recognise that certain states, such as China and India are becoming significant 'global players' (cf. ibid., p. 15). As those states increase in global power, the 2010 security strategy suggests that "(…) their ability to affect global issues (…)", as well as their "(…) military and other offensive capability" will develop as well (ibid.). This demonstrates that the UK considers other state's powers increasing as a relevant factor in the international system – although they are not perceived as factors which could pose immediate danger to national security. The UK's approach to the 'threat' of emerging powers is to strengthen its bilateral relationships with them (cf. ibid., p. 16). It is not mentioned whether the EU would be beneficial in this process. However, there is also no indication that the EU-membership would be a major obstacle either, justifying a referendum.

While it is emphasised that there are no immediate threats from other states, one further factor that could point to the awareness of an anarchic system is the constant systemic changes that are occurring in the world as emphasised in the strategy as follows:

> "The world will change. Our National Security Strategy needs to position us for the future as well as the present. We must scan the horizon, identify possible future developments, and prepare for them. We must be prepared for alternative futures based on key trends (…)" (ibid., p. 15).

This shows that the UK is aware of a certain level of 'unpredictability' in the international system. Under the conditions of anarchy in the international system, the UK recognises that somewhat unexpected developments could potentially happen in the space of a short time, since there is no higher authority, which could prevent potentially harmful or threatening developments. However, again there is no indication that the UK intends to protect itself against these threats by wanting to leave the EU. On the contrary, the strategy again highlights the significance of the EU in the international system (cf. ibid., p. 15). It can also be noted that the role of the EU will develop as well (cf. ibid.) possibly indicating that the UK based its partnership with the EU on the premise that the EU would develop over the years to be more efficient.

The 2015 security strategy starts with a foreword by the Prime Minister at the time, David Cameron, who outlines the UK's overall threat perception as well as its approach to tackle said threats. The main threats that Cameron points out, with relevance to this analysis from a neorealist perspective, are: The rise in terrorism, the increased instability of the Middle East, and the 'Ukraine crisis', which was prevalent at the time (cf. National Security Strategy 2015, p. 5). Apart from the Ukrainian crisis, the perception of the main threats is similar to the 2010 strategy. One difference is the source the terrorist threat originates from – the 2010 strategy pinpointed the terrorist groups Al Qaeda, whereas the 2015 strategy sees ISIL as the terrorist group presenting the biggest threat (ibid., p. 5). Identifying another terrorist group as a main threat, indicates that the anarchic structure of the international system 'allows' for new terrorist threats to emerge. Cameron emphasises that in order to maximise its security within the anarchic international system the UK needs to follow an approach "(…) to deter state-based threats, tackle terrorism (…) and ensure we have the capability to respond rapidly to crises as they emerge" (ibid., p. 6), placing emphasis on developing and increasing the UK's military and intelligence capabilities (cf. ibid.). However, in the 2015 strategy, Cameron also accentuates that:

> "(…) Britain's safety and security depends not just on our own efforts but working hand in hand with our allies to deal with the common threats that face us all (…). When confronted by danger we are stronger together. So, we will play our full part in the alliances which underpin our security (…). We will work with our allies in Europe and around the world (…)" (ibid.).

Whilst he does not explicitly mention the 'EU', Cameron does imply that the European allies are important. Therefore, this does not show any clear indications that the UK is eager to hold a referendum on its EU-membership in order to maximise their security in the international system.

The 2015 security strategy is based on the UK's perception of the pace in which the world is changing, emphasising that the UK perceives there to be "(…) long-term shifts in the balance of global economic and military power, increasing competition between states, and the emergence of more powerful non-state actors" (ibid., p. 15). While this account is somewhat similar to the 2010 strategy, the 2015 strategy states that the threats the UK is facing are more complex now (cf. ibid.), thus indicating that there is a perception that anarchic system causes the complexity of potential security issues to increase, and therefore also increasing insecurity. As mentioned above, the major security threats that the 2015 strategy identifies, relevant for this analysis of the perception of external threats in an anarchic international system, form a neorealist perspective are: Terrorism and instability, as well as increasing state-based threats (cf. ibid.).

Again, the threat of terrorism is classified as being the most potent one, although the focus is now on the terrorist group ISIL, who predominantly originates from Syria and Iran (cf. ibid., p. 16) – as a result of instability in the overall region caused by "(…) conflict in Syria and Iraq (…)" (ibid.). Further, the strategy emphasises that the threat has increased, due to different methods employed by terrorist groups (cf. ibid., p. 37). In order to combat the growing threat of terrorism that UK's prime approach is to "(…) increase the resources for counter-terrorism policy and the security and intelligence agencies to pursue terrorists" (ibid., p. 38). This resource increase is restricted to domestic factors in the UK – the UK is not necessarily relying on other states or institutions on this matter. However, the strategy also states that the UK "(…) will continue to work with close allies and partners including NATO and the EU (…)" (ibid., p. 39). This approach shows that the UK does consider the EU to be a valuable partner in the fight against terrorism, thus indicating that there was no clear demand for a referendum on its EU-membership, due to the increased security threat.

The second major threat the 2015 strategy identifies, is the intensification of threats originating from other states. While the 2010 strategy mainly focused on the spread of nuclear proliferation of states, such as Iran, and the resulting threats, the 2015 strategy specifically asserts that "(…) Russia has become more aggressive, authoritarian and nationalist, increasingly defining itself in opposition to the West" (ibid., p. 18), thus indicating that another state poses a concrete threat. The strategy does also refer to nuclear threats, indicating that Russia has been increasing "(…) its nuclear exercises and rhetoric (…)" (ibid.). The anarchic system allows Russia to behave in such a way that the UK perceives it as a potential threat. The strategy states that "Russia's behaviour will continue to be hard to predict, and, though highly unlikely, we cannot rule out the possibility that it may feel tempted to act aggressively (…)" (ibid.). In order to maximise its security, the UK identifies NATO as its prime partner since "(...) NATO's commitments include the Allies' defence investment pledge and the Readiness Action Plan, which respond to the challenges posed by Russia (…)" (ibid.). The EU does not seem to play an important role in the defence against the 'Russian threat'. Although it has been sanctioning Russia (ibid.), these sanctions only happened because the UK urged the EU to do so (ibid.) – perhaps indicating the UK's dissatisfaction with the EU in dealing with Russia.

Both strategies, especially 2015's, emphasise the importance of the UK's relationship with NATO in security and defence matters. This could indicate that the UK did not classify the EU as a necessary partner in those matters which could have been a contributing factor to the referendum decision, but this is purely conjecture. The results of the analysis do not suggest that the insecurity of the anarchic international system and its threats played a significant role in the referendum decision. However, there are other factors from a neorealist perspective that might have contributed to the referendum decision – the 'desire' to survive in the anarchic international system by maximising one's security through the means of 'self-help' and strategic thinking. These factors will be analysed in the subsequent chapters.

1.1.2. The 'Desire' to Survive in the International System Through Security Maximisation

Neorealism suggests that there is no higher entity that could guarantee protection in the insecure international system and states have to resort to 'self-help' in order to maximise their security – which is essential in ensuring a state's survival. This means states have to form their own strategies to achieve this maximum security as there is no one they could rely on. Waltz suggests that states can opt to choose between internal- and external power balancing to maximise their security. Achieving this 'balance of power' might deter aggressive states from acting aggressively towards other states. These strategy options present the basis for the subsequent analysis in an attempt to find indications that the 'desire to survive' through the 'self-help' concept played a decisive role in the UK's referendum decision. I first examine the strategy of internal balancing by looking at the UK's defence expenditures in the observational period, before analysing the UK's potential strategies that would imply external balancing, by again looking at the national defence strategies.

In his theory, Waltz identifies the increase of military capabilities as one of the main strategies of internal balancing for states in order to maximise their security in the inse- cure anarchic international system. Therefore, I examine the UK's domestic and interna- tional security strategies and defence expenditures in order to find evidence that the UK perceived the procuration of its own security in the international system as the highest priority.

The UK puts strong emphasis on the necessity of its military capabilities since the "(…) role of our Armed Forces is to defend the UK so that we can live in peace" (National security strategy 2015, p. 27) – placing its military at the centre of the defence efforts in order to maximise its security. When looking at the observational period relevant for this paper, from 2013 until 2016, the UK defence expenditures remained relatively balanced with no significant in- or decreases (cf. Dempsey2018, p. 4). Throughout this period the defence expenditures roughly ranged from 34,3 pounds billion to 35,1 billion pounds (ibid.), indicating no noteworthy changes. The UK Ministry of Defence (MoD) also high- lights the fact that in general the trend, prior to the observational period as well as during it, shows a decrease in defence spending by stating that "(…) since 2011 defence expendi- ture has fallen in both real and actuals terms (…)" (Ministry of Defence 2017, p. 5). This would initially point to the fact that the UK's perception of an increased threat in the international system, as discussed in the previous chapter, does not lead it massively in- creasing its defence spending, therefore implying that the UK does not pursue self-help through enhanced military armament. This notion is supported by a report published by the House of Commons regarding the UK's defence expenditures. The report states that:

> "The last Strategic Defence and Security Review (SDSR) in 2010 resulted in
> a reduction of 8% in defence spending. This led in turn to a 20% reduction in
> the UK's conventional military combat capability. In 2013, with the UK GDP
> at £1.61 trillion and a defence budget of £37.1 billion, defence expenditure
> totalled 2.30% of GDP. By 2014, UK GDP was £1.7 trillion, the defence
> budget had fallen to £36.9 billion, just 2.17% of GDP (…)" (2016, p. 4).

This demonstrates the UK has been placing little emphasis on increasing its military ca- pabilities over the last decade. In terms of the referendum decision, this could indicate that the UK did not increase its military spending since its EU-membership would help it in procuring its national security. However, as has been established above, the EU does not play a huge role in the UK's defence strategies. This is emphasised by Whitman, who accentuates that the "(…) UK's foreign security and defence policy has never been solely pursued through the EU but via a variety of institutions (most notably the North Atlantic Treaty Organization and the United Nations) and key bilateral relationships (…)" (2016a, p. R44). The fact that the UK does not see the EU as a central part of their defence and security matters could be a factor that played a role in the referendum decision.

After the initial examination of the data regarding the UK's defence expenditures, it could be assumed that internal balancing is not one of the strategies pursued to maximise the UK's security in the anarchic international system. However, when put in a different context, this assumption is questionable. When compared to the other European countries, "(…) the UK spends significantly more than any other EU member (…) in terms of defence expenditure (…)" (Duke 2019, p. 40). Furthermore, Duke emphasises that in 2014, the UK was one of only four countries who met the 2 per cent target set forth by NATO (ibid.). This target is "(…) a pledge by NATO's member states to aim at spending 2 percent of their respective gross domestic income (GDP) on defence within a decade" (Techau 2015, p. 3). Due to NATO being of high relevance in the UK's defence and security plans it could be said that they do place emphasis on internal balancing as a matter of self-help – through NATO. However, this further indicates that the EU seems irrelevant in the internal balancing strategy, which in turn could be interpreted as having an effect on the referendum decision. The UK's strong relationship with NATO and the resulting defence expenditures of the UK can be seen as a form of internal balancing to maximise the security and secure the 'survival' in the international system – however, it can also be seen as a strategy of external balancing. This will be examined in the subsequent chapter.

The Effects of External Balancing on the Referendum Decision

As established above, the UK's expenditures regarding security and defence are heavily influenced by the '2 per cent target' set by NATO – with UK's 2015 security strategy stating that "we will continue to meet the NATO target to invest 2% of GDP on defence

(…)" (National Security Strategy 2015, p. 27). However, the UK was also committed to defence and security policies within the EU – those being the Common Foreign and Security Policy (CFSP) and the Common Security and Defence Policy (CSDP). The CFSP's task is to coordinate the foreign policies of the member states, with each member state having the power to veto decisions made on a collective basis (Whitman 2016b, p. 257). However, due to the fact that the CFSP is reliant on intergovernmental cooperation, the UK has always been hesitant to participate (ibid.) and has opposed multiple reforms of the CSFP "(…) such as introducing qualified majority voting for decision-making (…)" (ibid.). Additionally, Whitman claims that the UK "(…) does not accept the proposition that member states should converge on a 'single' foreign policy that would replace those of the member states" (ibid., p. 258). This suggests that the UK is hesitant to take part and commit to the EU security and defence institutions due to the 'fear' of losing its autonomy. In terms of external balancing, this could imply that in order to maximise its security in the international system the UK strives to form an alliance without 'giving up' a lot of its autonomy in defence and security matters.

The CSDP "(…) focuses on preventing, managing and resolving conflict using both military and civilian resources" (Whitman 2016b, p. 258) – providing efficient external balancing that could help maximise a state's security. The CSDP has different intentions than NATO though (cf. ibid.). NATO emphasises the "(…) collective defence of its members and brings the military capabilities of the United States together with twenty-seven other states into a transatlantic military alliance (…)" (ibid.). Given the scope of NATO's capabilities it seems logical to pursue strategic balancing through investing in the membership to achieve the maximum 'amount' of security in the international system.

One of the central factors of the CSDP is that it depends on members to volunteer their forces for operations, as the EU does not have a defence budget (ibid.). The UK, however, has always "(…) been more keen on building bilateral defence relationships (outside the EU framework) (…)" (ibid.). This indicates that the UK did not determine the EU-defence institutions as relevant in its security and defence policies and in maximising its security in the international system but chose other strategic means to achieve this security. Supporting this notion is that the 2015 strategy does not mention the CSDP as a relevant factor in the UK's security and defence policies, but instead completely puts the focus on the UK's NATO commitments. The UK seems to focus on NATO as it has long-standing relationships with NATO and other states. The 2015 strategy supports this assumption by emphasising that "the security and stability of the UK has long depended on our strong partnerships in the Euro-Atlantic area, including NATO" (National Security Strategy 2015, p. 50). Furthermore, Whitman states that "relative to its size, the UK has been a very modest contributor to the military strand of the CSDP operations (…)" (2016b, p. 258). He continues to say that the UK has always preferred to commit to NATO (cf. ibid.). This sentiment is confirmed by Hill who asserts that "(…) the UK has always been nervous about the emerging tole of the EU in security and defence, fearing for a disruptive impact on NATO (…)" (Hill 2019, p. 56).

It is evident that the 2015 strategy is aimed at the cooperation with NATO or allied states, indicating that the UK intended to maximise its security through external balancing strategies that do not include the EU. The report of the House of Commons Defence Committee supports this, articulating that the UK government is committed to reach the 2 per cent NATO goal (cf. House of Commons 2016, p. 7), since "(…) this sends an important message to all the UK's partners and potential adversaries" (ibid.).

Further, the 2015 security strategy asserts that the UK expects its armed forces to be deployed "(…) with allies such as the US and France, through NATO; or as part of a broader coalition" (National Security Strategy 2015, p. 29). Throughout the whole 2010 and 2015 security strategies, great emphasis is placed on cooperating with NATO as well as France and the USA on matters of defence and security. The same can be said for the report by the House of Commons on the defence expenditures as well as the report by the MoD which were analysed throughout the course of this chapter. This indicates that in order to combat the insecurity of the anarchic system by maximising its national security, the UK attempts to achieve a 'balance of power' by placing the emphasis of its security and defence policies on the cooperation with NATO or other alliances, while at the same time disregarding the EU institutions. This could be an indicator that 'supports' the referendum decision because it shows that the UK was somewhat opposed to those EU institutions and never saw them as important in the security maximisation process.

1.2. Analysis from a Liberal Perspective

In this chapter, Moravcsik's liberal theory is used to analyse the referendum decision by considering domestic factors in the UK – namely, the societal actors as well as the role of domestic institutions and structures. I begin by placing the focus on the societal actors – those being private and other organised groups or individuals. Secondly, I analyse the role that political actors might have played. The final part of the analysis focuses on domestic institutions and structures in the UK and the influence they might have had on the referendum.

1.2.1. The Role of Societal Actors in the Referendum Decision

First, the focus is placed on some of the most significant interest groups with economic incentives and intentions, their preference formation and how they intended to pursue those preferences through political means. Secondly, I look at the part that these preferences of individual and collective political actors might have played in the referendum decision.

The Role of Interest Groups with Economic Incentives in the Referendum Decision

The interest groups with business and economic incentives relevant to this analysis are the Confederation of British Industry (CBI) as well as the biggest trade Union in the UK at the time 'Unite: the Union' (henceforth referred to as: Unite). During the observational period of this paper, the CBI released two documents illustrating its preferences regarding the UK's EU-membership. The first was published in 2013, titled 'Our Global Future' and the second in 2015, titled 'Choosing Our Future'. Both will be analysed to identify the CBI's preferences regarding an EU referendum and whether it might have influenced the referendum decision. Unite published relevant papers regarding their overall policies which address their preferences and goals as well, in 2012, 2014 and 2016. I analyse these publications in order to identify and provide a comprehensive summarised account of Unite's preferences regarding the referendum decision.

The CBI's 2013 paper is a publication aimed at illustrating its visions for the UK in the EU. The paper states that the "(…) UK's trading relationship with the European Union will remain of great importance regardless of the nature of formal relations" (Confederation of British Industry 2013, p. 9) and that "Britain does not face an 'either/or' choice – it needs to maximise trade with existing large markets at the same time as building links to new markets" (ibid.). This shows the significance the CBI attributes to the importance of remaining in extensive trading markets and expanding to new markets. The CBI highlights that the unified single market, provided by the EU, has improved the ability of businesses in the UK to increase their competitiveness (cf. ibid., p. 11), "(…) as well es bring them into complex European supply chains (…)" (ibid.), which enables them to significantly improve their exports (cf. ibid.). In a similar vein, the CBI also emphasises that the UK's EU-membership has made it easier for other European or indeed global partners to invest into UK businesses. These investments helped to "(…) start up factories, build office space (…) or support innovation in creative industries" (ibid.). The CBI underscores the EU's positive influence on the UK and its citizens in stating that the "(…) benefits arising from the EU membership is somewhere in the region of 4-5% of UK GDP (…)", which in turn "(…) suggests that households benefit from EU membership to the tune of nearly £3,000 a year (…)" (ibid.). This accentuates that the CBI considers the benefits of the EU to be relatively high.

While the overall tone of the CBI's paper is generally favourable of the UK's EU-membership, it does point out some criticism. Even though the benefits for UK businesses through the single open market of the EU have been substantial, the CBI emphasises that "(…) pressures on local services and wider public perceptions threaten to reduce the legitimacy of a vital element of the EU membership for business" (ibid., p. 11). The CBI feels that the principle of free movement of labour within the EU (cf. ibid.) needs to be reformed in a manner that allows it to "(…) continue to operate at a practical level for member states in the now enlarged and more economically diverse EU" (ibid.). Another issue the CBI sees with the EU is "(…) the UK's lack of unilateral control over regulation" (ibid.), although they are again in favour of seeing EU reforms, on "(…) poorly thought-out and costly EU legislation (…)" (ibid.). To address these issues, the CBI's preference is an adjustment to these principles to make it more fitting to the current constellation of the EU – suggesting reforms, not a referendum.

Overall, the 2013 CBI paper can be summarised by their statement that while "(…) UK membership of the EU has always had advantages and disadvantages" the benefits for the UK "(…) have been extensive" (ibid.). They also state that "business wants the UK to remain a member in the EU" (ibid., p. 162), underlined by the statistic that "71% of CBI member businesses reported that the UK's membership of the EU has had a positive overall impact in their business" (ibid., p. 11).

Up to this point the analysis shows no evidence indicating that the CBI could have played a major role in the referendum decision by aggregating the individual preferences of the decisions-makers of the UK's businesses. Rather, the preferences are 'pro-EU'. This could point to Moravcsik's assumption that societal actors, in this case the CBI as an interest group, are rational and averse to taking risks. The fact that the majority of the CBI members has largely benefited from the UK's membership in the EU implies a certain level of rationality since businesses achieved gains that outweigh the costs.

Analyses of the CBI's 'Choosing our Future' (2015) Publication Regarding its Preferences

In 2015 the CBI released another report indicating its preferences towards a referendum regarding the UK's EU-membership. Similar to the 2013 report, the 2015 reports states that "(…) the majority of firms believe that the 'pros' of EU-membership outweigh the 'cons'" (CBI 2015, p. 2) – suggesting that they are still in favour of the UK's EU-membership. Furthermore, the CBI does also maintain the stance that the "(…) the EU is far from perfect" (ibid.) and "(…) has its disadvantages" (ibid.) – one of the most significant being that it relies on compromises between countries which might interfere with the UK's individual objectives (ibid.). Building on this, the 2015 report again emphasises the need for reforms in the EU, especially from a legislative perspective. The report states that "aspects of EU legislation do get in the way of business" (ibid.). If the EU were to implement reforms and re-design the rules, the CBI believes that these would be "(…) powerful ways to support businesses to grow" (ibid., p. 11) The CBI has been adamant on promoting this agenda to reform the EU (cf. ibid.), because the "(…) majority of businesses want to remain in a reformed EU" (ibid., p. 2).

However, as in the 2013 report, the CBI sees these EU reforms as a necessity, but the general perception of the EU is still beneficial. The report also highlights the many benefits that the UK business sector receives by the UK's EU-membership stating that "(…) the European Union helps British businesses to grow and create more jobs across the UK (…)" (ibid.), as well as giving them "(…) access to over 500 million costumers" (ibid.). The report further indicates that this is hugely beneficial for UK businesses, highlighting the perceived benefits of the UK's membership in the EU. The CBI report emphasises that, through its EU-membership the UK can benefit from "(…) good quality trade deals which remove more barriers than most other trade deals" (ibid., p. 8) and that this would not be possible, if the UK had to negotiate these deals on its own (cf. ibid.). The analysis for the CBI's 2015 report makes it evident that business preferences have not changed significantly since 2013 – remaining in favour of a continued membership of the UK in the EU, albeit under the condition that the EU is reformed.

Analysis of the of the Trade Union 'Unite' Regarding its Preferences

The trade union 'Unite' is another interest group which could have played a role in the referendum decision. According to Jensen and Snaith, trade unions have always played a vital part in the UK's EU policy decisions (cf. 2016, p. 1305). However, due to the fact that they do not have strong ties to the UK's Conservative party, as the CBI does, they generally do not have much leverage (cf. ibid.). Unlike the CBI, Unite did not publish extensive papers, explicitly outlining its preferences regarding the UK's EU-membership. They published papers regarding their overall policies which include their preferences and goals as well. The analysis summarises publications from 2012, 2014 and 2016 in order to provide a comprehensive account of Unite's preferences and in turn the aggregated rational preferences of its individual members of the union.

The 2012 policy paper positions Unite as 'pro-EU', while also emphasising that it is opposed to alterations to the EU Treaty which will result in "(…) locking EU member states into austerity, cause further social and economic damage and hinder recovery" (Unite the

Union 2012, p. 32). This points to Unite criticising certain aspects of the EU. However, Unite does support the UK's EU-membership stating that "(…) UNITE is also fully opposed to any attempt to leave the European Union" (ibid.). Unite believes that leaving the EU would have severe negative economic consequences (cf. ibid.) as well as "(…) breaking away from an entity that has helped ensure peace on the European continent (…) and which has ushered many social and economic rights for UK workers" (ibid.). This indicates that the preferences of Unite are strongly directed at the UK's continued EU-membership.

The 2014 policy report indicates Unite's continued support of the UK's EU-membership. It states that "(…) Britain is better off within the EU than if would be if we left (…)" (2014, p. 20). However, the report does again indicate Unite's criticism regarding the EU, such as "(…) undermining collective bargaining and wage levels (…)" (ibid.), through different legislations. Nonetheless, the general preference of Unite is favourable towards the UK's EU-membership as the report conclusively states that Unite would "(…) argue for a vote for Britain to stay in the EU (…) while also campaigning against the neo-liberal agenda being promoted from Brussels" (ibid., p. 21). This indicates that Unite's aggregated preferences are supportive of the UK being an EU-member, however, it also identifies 'room for improvement'. Again, from the analysis of the 2014 report, no evidence can be identified indicating a significant role of Unite in the referendum decision.

Unite's 2016 report was released after the Brexit referendum was held. However, the report states that throughout the period in the run-up to the referendum, Unite strongly "(…) campaigned for Britain to stay in the EU as being in the best interests of the union's membership, particularly in terms of job security and worker's rights" (2016, p. 13). This indicates that since the previous major policy report in 2014, Unite's preference, and in turn the aggregated individual preferences of its members, remained stable up until the referendum, supporting the UK's EU-membership.

The CBI's and Unite's Attempt to pursue their Preferences through Political Means

An elementary part of Moravcsik's liberal theory is that societal actors, after forming their preferences, pursue those through political means to influence policy decisions. Here I will attempt to identify how the CBI and Unite tried to pursue their preferences regarding the UK's EU-membership by influencing the political process and thereby affecting the referendum decision. I look at a selected number of occasions potentially providing evidence regarding the CBI's and Unite's preference pursuit.

One way in which societal actors can try to advance their preferences through political means is by having good relationships with political parties. The CBI, as a significant representative of the business sector has "(…) traditionally strong ties to the Conservative party (…)" (Jensen and Snaith 2016, p. 1305). This means that the CBI would certainly 'target' David Cameron to push its preference as he was the leader of the Conservative Party as well as Prime Minister. In general, "the CBI has been careful to cultivate good relations with senior ministers in Government including the Prime Minister (…)" (On Mon 2013). Through its strong relationship with the Conservative Party, the CBI tried to pressure Cameron to figure out a way for the UK to stay in the EU (cf. Jensen and Snaith 2016, p. 1305). The CBI's president that time, Sir Mike Rake, exclaimed a referendum would cause major problems for the UK (cf. Dickie 2014). Rake addressed the Prime Minster, "(…) accusing him of causing uncertainty" and "real concern" for businesses" (ibid.). The CBI is against the UK leaving the EU and thus attempts to convey this preference directly to the Prime Minister by insinuating that his actions would have severe consequences. This pressure could then cause the Prime Minister to change his approach or attitude with regards to the referendum decision, which would favour the CBI's position.

In 2014 the director-general of the CBI at the time, John Cridland, called on British "(…) politicians not to wreck the country's 'best economic launch pad in 20 years' as they battle it out in the run-up to next year's general election" (Groom and Parker 2014). Furthermore, Cridland advised the politicians "(…) to spend the next nine months taking decisions that sustain the economic recovery rather than playing politics" (ibid.). This shows that the CBI attempts to influence the political process by drawing attention to issues that affect their preferences, such as economic stability, which could be threatened, if the UK were to leave the EU (cf. ibid). One prominent way in which the CBI attempts to convey and pursue its interests is through statements and demands made in the media. Similarly, in 2015, Sir Mike Rake spoke at a CBI event at which "(…) 1,000 businessmen and women, and politicians" (BBC 2015a) were present. Rake asserted that "in the months to come, our country will have to make its own choice. A choice between openness and isolation, between shaping the future or retreating into the past" (ibid). This shows the CBI's preference for the UK to remain an EU-member. Rake also elaborates that there is need for reform in the EU and that the CBI is in favour of the UK being the driving force behind those reforms (cf. ibid.).

Conversely, the trade unions in the UK do not have a particularly strong relationship with the Conservative party, making it more difficult for them to push their preferences through political means (cf. Jensen and Snaith 2016, p. 1305). However, for them the media is still a 'powerful' tool through which they can express their preferences and exert pressure to implement those into the political process. This is evident by the fact that the Trade Union Congress (TUC), which represents a large number of the trade unions in the UK, issued a statement in which it "(…) called on the Prime Minister to come clean about his plans for the re-negotiation of rights for working people (…)" (Trade Union Congress 2015). Furthermore, the TUC emphasised that Cameron would have to be honest about his intentions for the re-negotiations with the EU (cf. ibid.). This shows that the TUC pursues its preferences by calling on Cameron to be clear about his intentions, thus applying pressure through issuing demands via the media.

Another strategy employed by Unite was a certain level of blackmail to create leverage. One of Unite's biggest concerns about the EU was the potential weakening of worker's rights in the UK, hence they were supportive of reforms which would strengthen them. However, they feared that Cameron could potentially use "(…) his renegotiation with Brussels to weaken workers' rights" (O'Connor and Pickard 2015). Resulting from these concerns, Len McCluskey, who was Unite's general secretary at the time, (cf. ibid.), 'threatened' to "(…) switch sides and campaign to leave the EU" (ibid.), albeit being supportive of the UK's EU-membership. McCluskey emphasised that his "(…) union is a pro-Europe union [but] if Cameron was successful and watered-down workers' rights, I believe my union would need to seriously consider its position" (ibid). This shows that Unite attempted to pursue its individual aggregated preferences through putting pressure on the Prime Minister. The fact that Unite had over one million members at the time (cf. ibid.) which in turn are one million individual preferences, is an important factor in creating leverage for the pursuit of its preferences.

The Role of Individual and Collective Political Actors in the Referendum Decision

Based on the examined evidence, interest groups did not play a significant role in the referendum decision. Therefore, it seems plausible that other factors had an influence. Moravcsik's liberal theory suggests that the preferences of political, individual, or collective actors, also affect a state's foreign policy decision. These factors will now be examined.

The Preferences of David Cameron in the Referendum Decision

One of the major 'milestones' in the referendum decision is Cameron's, previously mentioned 'Bloomberg speech', in which he outlined his preferences regarding the UK's future relationship with the EU. Cameron emphasises that he sees a "(…) positive vision for the future of the European Union. A future in which Britain wants and should want to play a committed and active part" (UK Government 2013). However, the speech also outlines that Cameron is not satisfied with the nature of the UK's EU-membership as he aims for "(…) better deal for Britain" (ibid.). This shows that Cameron wants a re-negotiation of the UK's terms with the EU. He points out that there are three main challenges, which the EU faces (cf. ibid.) – those being the future of the Eurozone, the EU's future competitiveness and a certain loss of sovereignty due to EU-decision-making (cf. ibid.). Cameron emphasises that these challenges need to be dealt with, because otherwise "(…) the British people will drift towards the exit" (ibid.). However, Cameron also highlights his preference by stating that: "I do not want that to happen. I want the European Union to be a success (…)" (ibid.).

This shows that Cameron wants for the UK to remain in the EU, while also perceiving some issues asserting that the EU needs "(…) fundamental, far-reaching change" (ibid.). Cameron outlines that these changes need to address five key areas: competitiveness, flexibility, regaining of a certain level of sovereignty and power for member states, democratic accountability, and increased fairness (cf. ibid.). Cameron acknowledges that the British public perceive these problems with the EU and therefore expresses his "(…) favour of a referendum (…)" (ibid.). However, he strongly underscores his preference of the UK staying in the EU by stating "(…) that Britain's national interest is best served in a flexible, adaptable and open European Union (…)" (ibid.). This evidence indicates that Cameron's personal preference was the UK's continued membership in a reformed EU, however he also wants to give the British public the opportunity to have their say on the issue, thus calling for a referendum.

The 'referendum promise' as well the re-negotiations for EU reforms were contingent on Cameron being re-elected as Prime Minister in the 2015 general election. Cameron stated "(…) that his Conservative party would campaign for the parliamentary election on a promise to renegotiate the terms of Britain's EU membership" (Osborn and Griffiths 2013). Cameron also stated that he would invest everything into a "(…) campaign to keep Britain inside a reformed European Union (…)" (UK Government 2015), indicating that his preferences were still 'pro-EU'. He does also point out that, if the re-negotiations are largely unsuccessful the UK's EU-membership will have to be re-considered (cf. ibid.). Conclusively, it can therefore be said that Cameron's overall preference is for the UK to be a member of a reformed EU, but he wants to offer the British people the opportunity to vote on this matter. He believes that his re-negotiations with the EU regarding a better deal with the EU would result in a 'pro-EU' outcome.

The Conservative Party's and UKIP's Preferences Regarding the Referendum Decision

It seems plausible that the Conservatives, Cameron's party, and UKIP, as a highly 'anti-EU' party, are the two most relevant collective political actors that might have influenced the referendum decision due to "(…) Eurosceptic Conservatives continuing to push for a referendum on membership and UKIP rising (…)" (Schimmelfennig 2018, p. 1163). Their respective preferences will be analysed by examining their party manifestos within the observational period.

In order to analyse the preferences of the Conservative Party, I examine the 2014- and 2015-party manifestos. The 2014 manifesto was published in the run-up to the 2014 European Elections. It states that the party promises to hold a referendum on the UK's EU membership to 'restore' the UK's sovereignty (cf. The Conservative Party 2014, p. 3). The manifesto emphasises that the Conservatives want the UK to be "(…) part of a European Union – but whose interests, crucially, are guaranteed whether inside the Euro or out" (ibid., p. 15). Furthermore, it objects to an "(…) ever closer union (…)" (ibid.) and "(…) to unnecessary interference" (ibid.). To combat these issues, the Conservatives declare that they will give the British people the chance to vote on the UK's future in the EU (cf. ibid.). Furthermore, it is emphasised that the Conservatives are the only party that can actually deliver an 'in or out' referendum (cf. ibid., p. 20). In general, it can be said that the 2014 manifesto is rather 'pro-EU', but this depends on reforms that must be implemented in the EU, which the Conservatives hope to achieve during a possible 're-negotiation-process'.

The 2015 manifesto points out several changes in the EU, concerning the UK's national interests, such as cutting the EU budget "(…) saving the British taxpayer £8.15 billion" (2015, p. 72). However, it is reasserted that there are still plenty of more things that need improving (cf. ibid.). The 'demands' regarding the aspects of the EU that need changing are congruent with those outlined in the 2014 manifesto above. The Conservatives want "(…) an EU that helps Britain move ahead, not one that holds (…)" (ibid., p. 73) it back. The evidence from the manifestos indicates that the aggregated individual collective preferences of the Conservative Party are favourable of the EU. However, major reforms within the EU, that would make the EU more appealing to the national interests of the UK, were also advocated. Furthermore, they wanted the British public to vote on the UK's EU-membership in an in/out referendum.

The other party, which undoubtedly played a significant role in the referendum decision, is UKIP. In order to analyse their preferences, their 2014 European election manifesto as well their 2015 general election manifesto are examined. UKIP is generally a Eurosceptic party. One of UKIP's biggest objectives is to 'regain control' (cf. UKIP 2014, p. 4) over the UK, which has been diminished by the EU, through its bureaucracy, among other things (cf. ibid.) or its control of aspects, such as "(…) immigration, law and order and energy (…)" (cf. ibid.). It believes that the UK can only achieve this by leaving the EU (cf. ibid.). One of the main issues UKIP outlines with the EU is the "loss of control" (ibid.) of its borders, which has resulted in high levels of migration to the UK (cf. ibid.). UKIP's 2014 manifesto states that the UK needs 'repairing' (cf. ibid., p. 7) in a significant number of areas which have been restricted or indeed 'damaged' (cf. ibid.) by the EU and the other UK parties, who are supportive of the EU-membership. It emphasises that "only by leaving the EU can we begin the process of undoing the damage (…)" (ibid.).

UKIP's 2015 manifesto largely echoes the claims and demands of the 2014 manifesto. It still strongly advocates the discontinuation of the UK's EU-membership (cf. UKIP 2015, p. 70). UKIP's 'anti-EU' preferences can be summarised effectively in the following quotation from their 2015 manifesto:

> "A British exit from EU, (…) is the only choice open to us, if we are to make our own laws and control our own destiny. Unless we leave, our democracy, our law-making powers and our sovereignty will continue to be salami-sliced away be the EU. Genuine reform is impossible" (ibid.).

Their preference is crystal clear: they want the UK to leave the EU. It also stresses that any reforms will be to no avail, whereas Cameron and the Conservatives strongly believe that those are key to the UK's continued EU-membership. Conclusively, it can be observed that the individual preferences of the UKIP members lead to an overall collective preference, represented by UKIP, that is for the UK to leave the European Union. These preferences are in conflict with Cameron's and the Conservative's preferences to remain in the EU, and to have reforms, however, it is not yet clear how those diverging preferences might have led to the referendum decision.

The Influence of Conflicts over Preferences Within- or Between the Political Actors on the Referendum Decision

There is evidence suggesting that conflicts within the Conservative Party and the Prime Minister, David Cameron, resulted in the UK's decision to call for a referendum on its EU-membership. The analysis of the potential conflicts can be split into two focal time periods – the first one roughly being the time of the Bloomberg speech in January of 2013 and the second one after the general election of Cameron in 2015. The analysis is based on statements, speeches, and accounts from newspapers and secondary literature.

The Influence of 'Inner-Party' Conflicts on the Referendum Decision

Within the Conservative Party, "the issue of EU membership became a running sore in the first half of the 2010 – 2015 (…)" (Smith 2016, p 328). One of the main problems for the Conservative party and indeed Cameron, were the, so called 'backbenchers' – members of the Conservative Party, who "(…) had been plotting from inside the Conservative Party, rebelling against their leaders trying to galvanize support for a Brexit on the backbenches in the House of Commons (…)" (Clarke et al. 2017, p. 15). The backbenchers were characterised by their strong Euroscepticism and their views that the Conservatives had continuously failed to reduce European integration as well as to call for a referendum on the UK's EU membership (cf. ibid.). The first evidence indicating this is from 2011, when there was talk of an EU-referendum and 79 MPs of the Conservative party cast their vote favourable of an EU-referendum (cf. Watt 2011). The continued 'anti-EU' attitude by the backbenchers is reiterated by the fact even though in 2013 Cameron "(…) promised to hold a referendum by 2017 (…) many of his MPs say his promise is not enough (…)" (Kirkup 2013). This shows that Cameron was under considerable pressure regarding the UK's EU-membership from backbenchers in his own party, who then also "(…) smelled blood (…)" (Jensen and Snaith 2016, p. 1304), due to the fact that UKIP was starting to rise (cf. ibid.). Some of these Conservative critics also later left the party to join forces with UKIP. In an attempt to appease the backbenchers, Cameron then pledged, during the Bloomberg Speech, that he would hold a referendum on the UK's future in the EU, if he were re-elected as Prime Minister in the 2015 general elections (cf. Smith 2016, p. 329).

Cameron's promise "(…) meant that the sceptics in his backbenches (…) would mostly remain silent until after the general election" (ibid.). However, Cameron's Bloomberg announcement did not completely silence the 'anti-EU' voices of the backbenchers. This is proven by the fact that in January of 2014, "(…) 95 Conservative backbench members of parliament signed a letter (…) calling for parliament to be able to block EU laws (…)" (Evans and Menon 2017, pp. 9 – 10). This demonstrates that, despite Cameron's re-negotiation promise, strong Euroscepticism and therefore a conflict of different preferences, was still present among the backbenchers of the Conservative Party, which certainly could have had a major impact on the referendum decision.

A further major example of the backbenchers exerting pressure on Cameron was in 2015, just a few months after the general election, when "(…) Eurosceptic Tories joined forces with opposition MPs to defy the prime minister on the rules surrounding an EU referendum" (Rigby 2015). This resistance against these rules was based on the 'fear' among the backbenchers that "(…) ministers might use the machinery of government to make the case for the UK's continued membership in the union" (ibid.). This is echoed by the statement that "Eurosceptic Conservative MPs see the referendum as a once in lifetime opportunity to secure their goal of removing Britain from the EU (…)" (cf. ibid.), going against the preferences of the Prime Minister and indicating an 'inner conflict' within the Conservative Party. Thus far, there is considerable evidence indicating that inner-party conflicts played a significant role in the referendum decision.

The Influence of Conflicts Among Political Actors on the Referendum Decision

One of the most pressing subjects, which Cameron initially did not identify in his Bloomberg speech, was the issue of migration (Evans and Menon 2017, p. 20), an issue that was central for the Conservative backbenchers, as well as for UKIP. Goodwin and Milazzo argue that "(…) public hostility towards immigration and anxiety over its perceived effects was a major predictor of support for Nigel Farage and the populist right" (2017, p. 451). The 2015 Conservative party manifesto suggests immigration as beneficial to the UK but acknowledges the need for a certain level of immigration control. This clashes with UKIP's preferences that the only way to regain the immigration control is to leave the EU completely, as outlined in its manifesto. This indicates that there are conflicts over societally relevant issues among political actors, which could have influenced the referendum decision.

Goodwin and Milazzo, for instance, argue that the 'root conflict' over immigration was propelled by the events of the refugee crisis of 2015 (2017, p. 455). On one side of the conflict was UKIP who emphasised in their manifesto to "(…) stop the flow of migrants – whether immigrants, refugees, or asylum seekers – coming to the UK" (Brinded 2015), indicating that UKIP are not in favour of the EU's 'open-door-policy' regarding refugees. One the other side of the conflict is David Cameron, who announced that the UK would take in 20,000 refugees (cf. Akkoc and Wilkinson 2015). However, there was pressure in the EU for the UK to accept more refugees, as other countries were struggling to accommodate the sheer number of refugees (cf. BBC 2015b). This put Cameron under pressure. He was forced to deal with the refugee crisis on a European level, which could potentially be beneficial to his bargaining position in the re-negotiations of the UK's EU-membership. At the same time, he had to make sure that a deal regarding the refugee crisis would not have a significant impact in the UK, as this would provide UKIP with further 'anti-EU' ammunition. Consequently, this would have made the pursuit of his preference, keeping the UK in a reformed EU, considerably more difficult. This suggests the conflict of interests and preferences between Cameron, as individual political actors, and UKIP could have influenced the referendum decision.

The re-negotiations with the EU regarding the UK's EU-membership seem to be another factor related to societal conflicts between political actors leading to foreign policy decisions, i.e., the UK announcing a referendum. Having been re-elected in the general election of 2015, Cameron now needed to fulfil his promise of holding an EU-referendum as well as pursue his objectives for the re-negotiation of the UK's EU-membership. Cameron's demands were based on his Bloomberg speech as well the Conservatives Party manifesto, however, he did not combine them all into one coherent 'demand-paper', which he would present to the EU (cf. Smith 2016, p. 331). This led to domestic conflict, with critics claiming that Cameron's demands were not explicit enough (cf. ibid.). Cameron eventually outlined the following demands in a letter to Donal Tusk, the European council president at the time: economic governance, sovereignty, competitiveness, and immigration (cf. Smith 2016, p. 331). However, the letter was again, not especially detailed (cf. Traynor 2015). Arguably, the most important objective, that had been the source of major domestic conflict, was 'immigration'.

Cameron's negotiations with the EU ended with a new deal, in February 2016. However, while the "(...) new deal accommodated (...) several of the British requests" (Fabbrini 2017, p. 4), the crucial reforms regarding the issues of immigration "(...) had been watered down" (Clarke et al. 2017, p. 24). While Cameron was satisfied with the deal, critics emphasised that the deal will "(...) do nothing to curb migration and will trigger years of benefits chaos" (Slack et al. 2016). This indicates that Cameron misjudged the significance of certain conflictual issues, especially 'immigration', which placed him in a 'losing position' of a societal conflict – as suggested by Moravcsik – since he was not able to deliver the deal that the people wanted. This position made it considerably more difficult to pursue his preference of the UK staying in the EU and likely influenced the referendum decision.

1.2.2. The Role of Institutions in the Referendum Decision

Moravcsik's liberal theory posits that domestic institutions and structures can also affect a state's foreign policy. He argues that the aggregated preferences of societal actors are represented in the way institutions are designed and implies that there is an unequal representation of societal groups which restricts their potential influence on institutions. It seems probable that the referendum decision was influenced by legal frameworks in an institutional context with foreign policy implications. One piece of UK legislation that potentially influenced the referendum decision, by representing societal actors' preferences, is the European Union Referendum Act 2015 (EURA). It provides the legal framework for the referendum, building on the Political Parties, Election and Referendum Act 2000 (PPERA) legal framework. Further, the Transparency of Lobbying, Non-party Campaigning and Trade Union Administration Act 2014 (henceforth: Lobbying Act), could provide evidence that not all societal actors receive the equal amount of representation, limiting the ability to significantly influence institutions.

The Influence of the European Union Referendum Act 2015 on the Referendum Decision

The PPERA is a piece of UK legislation which "(…) sets out the legal framework for the conduct of referendums in the UK (…)" (UK Parliament 2020), specifying that "each referendum still requires primary legislation to set the terms of the question and the franchise to be used, amongst other provisions" (Uberoi 2015, p.3). In terms of the UK's referendum decision, the EURA 2015 presents such a piece of legislation as it is "an Act to make provision for the holding of a referendum in the United Kingdom and Gibraltar on whether the United Kingdom should remain a member of the European Union" (UK Parliament 2015, p. 1). The act set out the specifics of the planned referendum on the UK's EU-membership and provided a legal basis for the referendum.

The question is, if the act represents the aggregated preferences of societal actors and if societal actors shaped it in such a way that their preferences are turned into a national interest, as posited by Moravcsik. The EURA 2015 was fully approved on the 17th December of 2015 (cf. ibid.) and was legally applicable from the 1st of February 2016. The Referendum was contingent on Cameron being re-elected as Prime Minister in the 2015 general elections. Following his re-election in 2015, he fulfilled his promise and pursued the referendum, which resulted in the EURA 2015 – approved in parliament with "(…) 316 votes to 53 (…)" (BBC 2015c). Considering that the majority of MPs voted in favour of the EURA, leads to the assumption that they felt that their preferences were represented by the act. Prior to the 2015 general election, the three strongest parties in the UK were the Conservatives, the Labour Party and the Liberal Democrats (BBC 2010). Following the 2015 general election only the Liberal Democrats moved down to the fourth strongest party (BBC 2015d). Based on this, it could be assumed that these parties had previously formulated preferences regarding the referendum decision, which were eventually re-flected in the EURA 2015. The preferences can be examined by looking at the respective 2015 manifesto for each respective party.

The preferences of the Conservatives have already been outlined throughout this paper. They were strongly in favour of the UK's continued membership in a reformed EU. The examination of Labour's 2015 manifesto also indicates that they were in favour of the UK remaining in the EU, asserting their priority "(…) is not to take Britain out of Europe" (The Labour Party 2015, p. 103). However, the manifesto also states that the Labour Party "(…) will legislate for a lock that guarantees that there can be no transfer of powers from Britain to the European Union without the consent of the British public through an in/our referendum" (ibid.). This indicates that Labour's preference is also to keep the UK in the EU, but that it also wants reforms regarding the level of national sovereignty. The Liberal Democrat's manifesto also emphasises its favourable position of the UK being in the EU. They want Britain to play "(…) a constructive part in the European Union" (Liberal Democrats 2015, p. 143). Similarly, to the other manifestos, the Liberal Democrats also assert that they are in favour of an in/out referendum to prevent a further loss of sovereignty from the UK to EU (cf. ibid., p. 149). The analysis of the manifestos indicates that the three parties share the same preference of the UK regaining sovereignty, as well there being a clear demand for an in/out referendum.

The EURA 2015 explicitly states that "a referendum is to be held on whether the United Kingdom should remain a member of the European Union" (UK Parliament 2015, p. 1). This is congruent with the preferences of all of the three major parties, who demanded a clear referendum. The parties formulated their preferences prior to voting on the approval of the EURA 2015, and by voting to approve the act, shows that they were satisfied with its formulation. This further shows that the EURA 2015 represents the preferences of societal actors. It can be argued that this institution or policy, that 'mirrors' the societal interests influenced the referendum decision, since it provided the legal provision and framework for the referendum to be held. Nonetheless, while the examination of the EURA 2015 shows that political actors, i.e., the major parties were able to influence this institution through their preferences, there is no indication that other societal actors, such as interest groups were able to do so equally. This suggests that there are institutional restrictions preventing those societal actors from promoting their interests and converting them into national interests, as suggested by Moravcsik in his liberal theory.

The Influence of Inequal Institutional Representation and Inequal Influential Capabilities of Societal Actors on the Referendum Decision

Thus far throughout this paper, the research has shown that interest groups, despite their own strong preferences, were not able to influence the referendum decision in the same way that parties or political actors were. The 2014 Lobbying Act could present a legal institution 'responsible' for this. In summary, the act "(…) introduced restrictions as to what companies and non-governmental organisations can say in the 12 months leading up to a general election (…)" (Francis 2018). Considering that the referendum decision was one of the central aspects discussed in the general election, indicates that interest groups were potentially restricted in their ability to influence decision-makers. This demonstrates a certain level of inequality through an institution, as interest groups cannot influence the political process the same way parties do. The CBI is an interest group which is excluded from this act (cf. Wintour 2014), while trade unions are negatively affected, by having a number of somewhat unrealistic restrictions imposed on them (cf. Hayes 2014) – such as the requirement "(…) to maintain a register of the names and addresses of its members (…)" (UK Parliament 2014, p. 42). Due to the complex nature of large trade unions, this an extremely difficult undertaking (cf. Hayes 2014). The restrictions imposed by the act "(…) could affect campaign activity ranging from phone banks to public events that unions organise (…)" (Pickard 2015), indicating the unequal representation of interest groups.

Although the examined material does not provide clear evidence that the 2014 Lobbying act specifically influenced and limited the interest group's ability to influence the EURA 2015 and the referendum decision, some theoretical assumptions by Dunleavy indicate that this certainly could have been the case. Dunleavy argues that when "(…) interest groups are battling against party A's commitments (…) they will face an uphill struggle to make any changes in the incumbent government's policies" (2018) and that "governing parties in the UK have a strong record of pushing through partisan commitments" (ibid.). This suggests that the interest groups, be it the CBI or Unite, were always going to have difficulties influencing the political actors, i.e., the parties, due to strong commitments to their manifestos. Furthermore, Dunleavy additionally argues that in the UK "(…) there are sharp inequalities in the capabilities of different social groups (…) to get effectively involved in official consultation and legislative processes" (ibid.). This in turn could indicate that despite institutional restrictions, some societal actors might be able to influence the national interests more effectively than others. This could certainly be true for parties, as societal actors, in the case of the referendum decision, as they were not subject to as much institutional restriction as, for instance, interest groups. However, whether interest groups were able to do this, thus playing a significant role in the referendum decision is not conclusively apparent.

VI. __Conclusions and Outlook__

This dissertation analysed the inducements behind the UK's decision to hold a referendum on its membership in the European Union from the theoretical perspective of Waltz's neorealism and Moravcsik's liberal theory of international relations. The objective was to find the extent to which Waltz's neorealism and Moravcsik's liberal theory are able to explain the UK's decision to hold a referendum on its EU-membership, by analysing an array an array of different text-based sources, such as position papers, speech transcripts, official government documents and newspaper articles through a qualitative content analysis.

Based on the analysis, the theoretical assumptions of Kenneth Waltz's theory of neorealism, examined in this paper, are not able to explain the UK's referendum decision. The first variable tested was the 'anarchy of the international system' and the resulting insecurity as a relevant factor, derived from the first hypothesis. The results of the analysis indicate that while the UK perceives an insecure international system, thereby acknowledging anarchy, this did not play a role in the referendum decision. The second variables tested the hypothesised effects of 'self-help and strategic thinking', achieved through a form of balancing, to pursue security maximisation in the international system. The initial analysis did not show that the UK pursued classic internal balancing. However, there was evidence that the UK does seem to employ an adapted form of internal balancing, by heavily committing to NATO and its target through domestic defence expenditures, to maximise its security. The EU does not play a significant role in the UK's internal balancing strategies. It could therefore be argued that neorealism's predicted behaviour is pursued by the UK in some form, however, there was no clear evidence suggesting a connection to the referendum decision. Similar evidence was found regarding the strategy of external balancing. The UK pursues a form of external balancing through strong strategic connections with NATO to maximise its security, neglecting the EU and its institutions. While this could point to the fact that the UK's external balancing strategies did influence the referendum decision, no evidence was found supporting this notion. Therefore, it can be said that Waltz's neorealism exhibits little 'explanatory power' to explain the UK's referendum decision.

The second part of the analysis utilised elements of Moravcsik's liberal theory to analyse the referendum decision. Moravcsik's theoretical implications, focusing on the domestic factors as determinants for state's foreign policies, offer significantly more 'explanatory power' to explain the referendum decision, than the neorealist approach. The analysis first tested the hypothesised role of societal actors in the referendum decision – first looking at interest groups with strong economic incentives and preferences, and secondly at the role of individual and collective political actors. The analysis focused on the CBI and Unite as interest groups with economic interests. Based on the examination of the evidence, I found that those interest groups did not play a significant part in the referendum decision. The analysis showed that both groups pursued 'pro-EU' preferences and expressed demands for EU-reforms, but there was no evidence indicating they wanted the UK to leave the EU. This points to Moravcsik's assumption of his liberal theory of collectively aggregated interests of individuals, within the CBI and Unite, which are being pursued by collective action through the CBI and Unite as interest groups. I also found that the interest groups attempted to pursue these preferences, through the political process, using a variety of strategies and methods – as suggested by Moravcsik's theory. It could be argued that their EU-reform preferences were initially pursued by Cameron, but he made those contingent on a referendum, which was against the interest groups' interests. As the referendum went ahead regardless of these preferences and pursuits, this confirms the evidence that interest groups did not play a vital role in the referendum decision.

Secondly, I looked at the role of David Cameron, The Conservative Party, and UKIP as individual and collective political actors. I found the 'pro-EU' preferences of Cameron and the Conservatives, and UKIP's 'anti-EU' positions preferences potentially played a part in the referendum decision. Further, I looked at how potential conflicts among political actors affected the referendum decision. The analysis showed that 'inner-party' conflicts within the Conservatives, caused by backbenchers, led to the blocking of Cameron's favourable EU preferences and pressuring to hold a referendum This indicates that conflicts between political actors significantly affected the referendum decision. Further, the analysis identified conflicts between Cameron, the Conservatives and UKIP over immigration issues, which put Cameron in a difficult position for his re-negotiations with the EU. Thus, the analysis indicated that societal actors and their conflicts over diverging interests and preferences influenced the referendum decision, which coincides with Moravcsik's theoretical assumptions, thus confirming the first liberal hypothesis.

The second 'liberal' variable tested hypothesised the role of institutions and structures in the referendum decision. The focus was put on institutions in a legal context – the PPERA 2000, the EURA 2015 and the 2014 Lobbying act. The analysis indicated that the EURA 2015, as a legal provision for the referendum, certainly represented the preferences of some societal actors – particularly the strongest UK parties at the time. Further, the analysis showed those preferences were formed prior to the passing of the legislation, indicating that the parties were able influence it – confirming Moravcsik's assumption that societal preferences are represented institutions, which certainly affected the referendum decision.

Lastly, the analysis focused on Moravcsik's assumption that some societal groups receive unequal representation from institutions. Examining the 2014 Lobbying Act showed that some societal actors are indeed restricted by institutions in their ability to influence the political process. The analysis showed that some societal groups, particularly parties and business interest groups arguably receive more representation, while groups, such as trade unions receive less. Therefore, the former groups are more able to influence the political process and national interests than, for instance, trade unions – congruent with Moravcsik's unequal representation assumption of societal groups through institutions. However, the analysis did not find conclusive evidence that these restrictions significantly contributed to the referendum decision. While the analysis was unable to confirm all of Moravcsik's theoretical assumptions regarding institutions having affected the referendum decision, some clear evidence was found suggesting so – thereby confirming the second liberal hypothesis.

The summarised results of the analysis show that Moravcsik's liberal theory offers a more comprehensive framework to explain the referendum decision than Waltz's neorealism. However, the examined sources have to be considered as well to consider the validity and reliability of the results. In terms of the validity of the analysis, it can be said that the examined sources were appropriately chosen in order to gain plausible results to answer the research question. The selection of the research variables was effective to test the effects of the relevant theoretical elements on the referendum decision. The main focus of the operationalisation on primary sources, such as manifestos, official security strategies, government documents, speeches, and newspaper articles, supported by secondary literature, certainly delivered convincing and appropriate results, in both analyses, to answer the research question. However, it also needs to be considered that the examination of other documents, especially regarding the analysis of the institutions, as well the focus on different societal groups in the liberal analysis, could potentially produce different results and lead to a different conclusion. Nonetheless, the analysis conducted produced satisfying results to answer the research question.

There seem to be other reasons, not discussed, and considered by Neorealism or Liberalism – such as the fundamental personal or national identities and motivations behind the actors' preferences and actions as well as other far-reaching complex economic incentives – which could provide additional insights into the reasons behind the referendum decision. Social constructivism in the field of international relations, is a theory which, could be used to analyse these factors in future studies, as it "(…) brings to the fore the importance of ideas, identity, and interaction in the international system (…)" (Collins 2016,

p. 71) and assumes the world surrounding us, not to be an unchangeable construct, but instead is shaped through the actions of the actors within it (cf. ibid.). These are areas into which future research could certainly be very insightful, considering the huge significance of the UK's referendum decision in laying the foundations for Brexit – one of the most remarkable events in recent European history.

VII. <u>Bibliography</u>

AKKOC, R. AND WILKINSON, M. (2015). 'David Cameron: Britain will accept 20,000 refugees'. *The Telegraph*, 7th September. Available at: https://www.telegraph.co.uk/news/worldnews/europe/11848150/Refugee-crisis-Syria-and-foreign-aid-budget-David-Cameron-in-Parliament-live.html (Accessed: 13th March 2020).

ASTHANA, A., QUINN, B. AND MASON, R. (2016). 'UK votes to leave EU after dramatic night divides nation'. *The Guardian*, 24th June. Available at: https://www.theguardian.com/politics/2016/jun/24/britain-votes-for-brexit-eu-referendum-david-cameron (Accessed: 20th Feb. 2020).

BBC (2010). 'Election 2010'. *BBC News*. Available at: http://news.bbc.co.uk/2/shared/election2010/results/ (Accessed: 16th March 2020).

BBC (2014). 'Unite to fund Labour to make election 'fair fight''. *BBC News*, 30th June. Available at: https://www.bbc.com/news/uk-28084222 (Accessed: 16th March 2020).

BBC (2015A). 'EU membership is in UK's national interest – CBI'. *BBC News*, 20th May. Available at: https://www.bbc.com/news/business-32805539 (Accessed: 13th March 2020).

BBC (2015B). 'David Cameron urges EU countries to follow UK's lead on refugees'. *BBC News*, 14th September. Available at: https://www.bbc.com/news/uk-34242346 (Accessed: 28th February 2020).

BBC (2015C). 'EU referendum: Cameron suffers Commons defeat over 'purdah' rules'. *BBC News*, 9th September. Available at: https://www.bbc.com/news/uk-politics-34173126 (Accessed: 2nd March 2020).

BBC (2015d). 'Election 2015'. BBC News. Available at: https://www.bbc.com/news/election/2015/results (Accessed: 3rd March 2020).

BBC (2016). 'EU referendum: Cameron sets June date for UK vote'. *BBC News*, 20th February. Available at: https://www.bbc.com/news/uk-politics-35621079 (Accessed: 16th March 2020).

BRINDED, L. (2015). 'The refugee crisis is going to blow Britain out of the European Union'. *Business Insider*, 7th September. Available at: https://www.businessinsider.com/the-refugee-crisis-is-going-to-blow-britain-out-of-the-european-union-2015-9?r=DE&IR=T (Accessed: 16th March 2020).

CLARKE, D., GOODWIN, M. AND WHITELEY, P. (2017). *Brexit: why Britain voted to leave the European Union*. Cambridge: Cambridge University Press.

COLLINS, A. (2016). *Contemporary security studies*. Oxford, United Kingdom: Oxford University Press.

CONFEDERATION OF BRITISH INDUSTRY (2013). *Our Global Future: The business vision for a reformed EU*. Confederation of British Industry: London. Available at: https://boardagenda.com/resource/global-future-business-vision-reformed-eu-2013/ (Accessed: 1st March 2020).

CONFEDERATION OF BRITISH INDUSTRY (2015). *Choosing Our Future: Why the European Union Is Good for Business, But How it Should be better*. Confederation of British Industry: London. Available at: https://urbis.europarl.europa.eu/urbis/sites/default/files/generated/document/en/http___news.cbi_.org_.uk_news_cbi-makes-case-for-being-in-a-reformed-eu_choosing-our-future_.pdf (Accessed: 16th March 2020).

CONFEDERATION OF BRITISH INDUSTRY (2020). *'About us'*. Available at: https://www.cbi.org.uk/about-us/ (Accessed: 13th March 2020).

DEMPSEY, N (2018). *UK Defence Expenditure*. London: House of Commons Library. Available at: https://commonslibrary.parliament.uk/research-briefings/cbp-8175/ (Accessed: 10th March 2020)

DICKIE, M. (2014). 'Cameron dismisses claim that euroscepticism fuels Scots Yes vote'. *Financial Times*, 29th August. Available at: https://www.ft.com/content/5bd79f72-2f8c-11e4-87d9-00144feabdc0 (Accessed: 16th March 2020).

DIEZ, T., BODE, I. AND FERNANDES, A. (2011). *Key concepts in international relations*. Los Angeles: Sage.

DUKE, S. (2019). *Will Brexit damage our security and defence?: the impact on the UK and EU*. Cham, Switzerland: Palgrave Macmillan.

DUNLEAVY, P. (2018). 'How democratic is the interest groups process in the UK?' *Democratic Audit UK*. Available at: https://www.democraticaudit.com/2018/08/24/audit2018-how-democratic-is-the-interest-group-process-in-the-uk/ (Accessed: 13th March 2020).

EVANS, G. AND MENON, A. (2017). *Brexit and British politics*. Cambridge, UK; Medford, Ma: Polity Press.

FABBRINI, F. (2017). *The law & politics of Brexit*. Oxford: Oxford University Press.

FRANCIS, S. (2018). 'The Lobbying Act is stifling charity campaigners. It doesn't have to'. *The Guardian*, 17th January. Available at: https://www.theguardian.com/voluntary-sector-network/2018/jan/17/the-lobbying-act-stifling-charity-campaigns-it-shouldnt (Accessed: 13th March 2020).

GLÄSER, J. AND LAUDEL, G. (2013). Theoriegeleitete Textanalyse? Das Potential einer variablenorientierten qualitativen Inhaltsanalyse. *Veröffentlichungsreihe der Arbeitsgruppe Wissenschaftstransformation des Wissenschaftszentrums Berlin für Sozialforschung (WZB)*, pp.99-401.

GOODWIN, M. AND MILAZZO, C. (2017). Taking back control? Investigating the role of immigration in the 2016 vote for Brexit. *The British Journal of Politics and International Relations*, 19(3), pp.450–464.

GROOM, B. AND PARKER, G. (2014). 'CBI warns politicians not to rock the boat'. *Financial Times*, 16th July. Available at: https://www.ft.com/content/95314d2c-0ceb-11e4-90fa-00144feabdc0 (Accessed: 15th March 2020).

GU, X. (2000). *Theorien der internationalen Beziehungen: Einführung*. Munich: Oldenbourg.

HAYES, B. (2014). 'The gagging bill looks designed to undermine trade unions'. *The Guardian*, 29th January. Available at: https://www.theguardian.com/commentisfree/2014/jan/29/lobbying-bill-trade-unions-law (Accessed: 12th February 2020).

HILL, C. (2019). *The future of British foreign policy: security and diplomacy in a world after Brexit*. Cambridge: Polity.

HOUSE OF COMMONS (2016). *Shifting the goalpost? Defence expenditure and the 2% pledge*. UK Parliament: London. Available at: https://publications.parliament.uk/pa/cm201516/cmselect/cmdfence/494/494.pdf (Accessed: 16th March 2020).

HUNT, A. (2014). 'UKIP: The story of the UK Independence Party's rise'. *BBC News*, 21st November. Available at: https://www.bbc.com/news/uk-politics-21614073 (Accessed: 12th March 2020).

JENSEN, M.D AND SNAITH, H. (2016). When politics prevails: the political economy of a Brexit. *Journal of European Public Policy*, 23(9), pp.1302-1310.

KIRKUP, J. (2013). 'Half of all Conservative backbenchers demand EU referendum law'. *The Telegraph*, 15th May. Available at: https://www.telegraph.co.uk/news/newstopics/eureferendum/10060550/Half-of-all-Conservative-backbenchers-demand-EU-referendum-law.html (Accessed: 5th March 2020).

LAYNE, C. (1993). The Unipolar Illusion: Why New Great Powers Will Rise. *International Security*, 17(4), pp.5-51.

MASALA, C. (2014). *Kenneth N. Waltz. Einführung in seine Theorie und Auseinandersetzung mit seinen Kritikern*. Baden-Baden: Nomos.

MAYRING, P. (2015). Qualitative Inhaltsanalyse: Grundlagen und Techniken. Weinheim and Basel: Beltz

MENDEZ, F. AND MENDEZ, M. (2017): Referendums on EU Matters. *European Parliament, Directorate-General for Internal Policies, Policy Department C, Citizen's Rights and Constitutional Affairs*. European Parliament: Brussels.

MINISTRY OF DEFENCE (2017). *Finance & Economic Annual Bulletin. Departmental Resources Statistics*. UK Government: London. Available at: https://assets.publishing.service.gov.uk/government/uploads/system/uploads/attachment_data/file/649443/Finance_and_economics_annual_statistical_bulletin_departmental_resources_2017.pdf (Accessed: 9th January 2020).

MORAVCSIK, A. (1997). Taking Preferences Seriously: A Liberal Theory International Politics, *International Organization*, 51(4), pp.513-553.

MORAVCSIK, A. (1998). *The choice for Europe: social purpose and state power from Messina to Maastricht*. Ithaca, New York: Cornell University Press.

MORAVCSIK, A. (2001). *Liberal international relations theory: a social scientific assessment*. Cambridge, Mass.: Harvard University, Weatherhead Centre for International Affairs.

MORAVCSIK, A. (2010). 'The New Liberalism', In: Reus-Smit. and Snidal, D. *The Oxford Handbook of International Relations*. Oxford: Oxford University Press, pp. 234-238.

MORRIS, N. (2013). 'Britain's biggest unions put weight behind plan for general strike'. *Independent*, 4th April. Available at: https://www.independent.co.uk/news/uk/politics/britains-biggest-unions-put-weight-behind-plan-for-general-strike-8559027.html (Accessed: 14th March 2020).

O'CONNOR, S. AND PICKARD, J. (2015). 'Britain's biggest union Unite weighs up campaigning for Brexit'. *Financial Times*, 16th July. Available at: https://www.ft.com/content/3aae1b92-2bac-11e5-8613-e7aedbb7bdb7#axzz3xR6yXJ7T (Accessed: 14th March 2020).

O'ROURKE, K. (2019). *A short history of Brexit: from Brentry to backstop*. London: Pelican.

ON MON, C. (2013). *A Look at CBI: The Powerful Voice of the UK Business. Association of Accredited Public Policy Advocates to the European Union*. Available at: http://www.aalep.eu/look-cbi-powerful-voice-uk-business (Accessed: 4th February 2020).

OSBORN, A. AND GRIFFITHS, P. (2013). 'Cameron promises Britons vote on EU exit'. *Reuters*, 23rd January. Available at: https://www.reuters.com/article/us-britain-europe/cameron-promises-britons-vote-on-eu-exit-idUSBRE90L16D20130123 (Accessed: 7th March 2020).

PICKARD, J. (2015). 'Unions say lobbying curbs will hit election campaigning'. Financial Times, 8th January. Available at: https://www.ft.com/content/79d18d36-9746-11e4-9636-00144feabdc0 (Accessed: 16th March 2020).

RIGBY, E. (2015). David Cameron suffers backbench rebellion on Europe. *Financial Times*, 7th September. Available at: https://www.ft.com/content/1ca72b70-5582-11e5-9846-de406ccb37f2 (Accessed: 5th March 2020).

SCHIEDER, S. (2010) 'Neuer Liberalismus', In: Schieder, S., Spindler, M. *Theorien der Internationalen Beziehungen*. Opladen: Budrich.

SCHIMMELFENNIG, F. (2018). Brexit: differentiated disintegration in the European Union. *Journal of European Public Policy*, 25(8), pp.1154–1173.

SCHÖRNIG, N. (2010). 'Neorealismus', In: Schieder, S., Spindler, M. *Theorien der Internationalen Beziehungen*. Opladen: Budrich.

SLACK, J., GROVES, J. AND STEVENS, J. (2016). 'The great delusion: PM hails EU 'reforms' but critics say they'll do nothing to curb migration and will trigger years of benefits chaos'. *The Daily Mail*, 3rd February. Available at: https://www.dailymail.co.uk/news/article-3429191/The-great-delusion-PM-hails-EU-reforms-critics-say-ll-curb-migration-trigger-years-benefits-chaos.html (Accessed: 10th March 2020).

SMITH, J. (2016). David Cameron's EU renegotiation and referendum pledge: A case of déjà vu? *British Politics*, 11(3), pp.324-346.

THE CONSERVATIVE PARTY (2014). *Conservative party European Election Manifesto 2014*. The Conservative Party: London. Available at: Directly downloadable PDF via Google Search. (Accessed: 16th March 2020).

THE CONSERVATIVE PARTY (2015). *The Conservative Party Manifesto 2015*. The Conservative Party: London. Available at: http://ucrel.lancs.ac.uk/wmatrix/ukmanifestos2015/localpdf/Conservatives.pdf (Accessed: 16th March 2020).

THE LABOUR PARTY (2015). *The Labour Party Manifesto 2015*. The Labour Party: London. Available at: https://action.labour.org.uk/page/-/A4%20BIG%20_PRINT_ENG_LABOUR%20MANIFESTO_TEXT%20LAYOUT.pdf (Accessed: 16th March 2020).

THE LIBERAL DEMOCRATS (2015). *Manifesto 2015 – Stronger Economy. Fairer Society. Opportunity for Everyone*. The Liberal Democrats: London. Available at:

https://d3n8a8pro7vhmx.cloudfront.net/libdems/pages/8907/attachments/origi-nal/1429028133/Liberal_Democrat_General_Election_Mani-festo_2015.pdf?1429028133 (Accessed: 15th March 2020).

TECHAU, J. (2015). The politics of 2 percent: NATO and the security vacuum in Eu-rope. Washington, DC: Carnegie Endowment for International Peace; Brussels, Belgium: Car-negie Europe.

THE NATIONAL SECURITY STRATEGY (2010). *The National Security Strategy – a strong Britain in an age of uncertainty*. UK Government: London. Available at: https://as-sets.publishing.service.gov.uk/government/uploads/system/uploads/attach-ment_data/file/61936/national-security-strategy.pdf (Accessed: 16th March 2020).

THE NATIONAL SECURITY STRATEGY (2015). *National Security Strategy and Strategic Defence Security Review 2015*. UK Government: London. Available: https://assets.pub-lishing.service.gov.uk/government/uploads/system/uploads/attach-ment_data/file/478933/52309_Cm_9161_NSS_SD_Review_web_only.pdf (Accessed: 16th March 2020.

TRADE UNION CONGRESS (2015). *TUC calls on Prime Minister to come clean about his plans to re-negotiate worker's rights from Europe*. Trade Union Congress: London. Available at: https://www.tuc.org.uk/news/tuc-calls-prime-minister-come-clean-about-his-plans-re-negotiate-workers-rights-europe (Accessed: 26th February 2020).

TRAYNOR, I. (2015). 'David Cameron's EU demands letter explained'. *The Guardian*, 10th November. Available at: https://www.theguardian.com/politics/2015/nov/10/david-camerons-eu-demands-letter-explained (Accessed: 12th March 2020).

UBEROI, E. (2015). *European Union Referendum Bill 2015-15*. House of Commons Li-brary: London. Available at: https://commonslibrary.parliament.uk/research-brief-ings/cbp-7212/ (Accessed: 1st March 2020).

UK GOVERNMENT (2013). EU speech at Bloomberg. UK Government: London. Available at: https://www.gov.uk/government/speeches/eu-speech-at-bloomberg (Accessed: 16th March 2020).

UK GOVERNMENT (2015). Prime Minster's speech on Europe. UK Government: London. Available at: https://www.gov.uk/government/speeches/prime-ministers-speech-on-europe (Accessed: 12th March 2020).

UK INDEPENDENCE PARTY (2014). *UKIP Manifesto 2014 – Create an earthquake.* UK Independence Party: Newton Abbot. Available at: https://d3n8a8pro7vhmx.cloudfront.net/themes/5308a93901925b5b09000002/attachments/original/1398869254/EuroManifestoLaunch.pdf?1398869254 (Accessed: 15th March 2020).

UK PARLIAMENT (2014). Transparency of Lobbying, Non-Party Campaigning and Trade Union Administration Act 2014. UK Parliament: London. Available at: http://www.legislation.gov.uk/ukpga/2014/4/pdfs/ukpga_20140004_en.pdf (Accessed: 12th March 2020).

UK PARLIAMENT (2015). European Union Referendum Act 2015. UK Parliament: London. Available at: http://www.legislation.gov.uk/ukpga/2015/36/pdfs/ukpga_20150036_en.pdf (Accessed: 16th March 2020).

UK PARLIAMENT (2020). *Chapter 5: The referendum campaign: practical issues.* UK Parliament: London. Available at https://publications.parliament.uk/pa/ld200910/ldselect/ldconst/99/9907.htm (Accessed: 16th March 2020).

UNITE: THE UNION (2012). *Winning Together. Decisions of the June 2012 UNITE Policy Conference.* Unite: the Union. Available at: https://resources.unitetheunion.org/media/1008/1008.pdf (Accessed: 16th March 2020).

UNITE: THE UNION (2014). *Hope: Jobs, Homes, Health. Summary of decisions of the July 2014 Unite Policy Conference.* Unite: the Union: London. Available at: https://unitetheunion.org/media/1500/decisions-of-the-policy-conference-2014.pdf (Accessed: 3rd March 2020).

UNITE: THE UNION (2016). *Summary of decisions of the 2016 Unite Policy Conference.* Unite: the Union: London. Available at: https://unitetheunion.org/media/1501/decisions-of-the-policy-conference-2016.pdf (Accessed: 16th March 2020).

WALTZ, N.K. (1997). Evaluating Theories. *American Political Science Review*, 91(04), pp.913-917.

WALTZ, N. K. (2010). *Theory of international politics*. Long Grove, Ill.: Waveland Press.

WATT, N. (2011). 'David Cameron rocked by record rebellion as Europe splits Tories again'. *The Guardian*, 25th October. Available at: https://www.theguardian.com/politics/2011/oct/24/david-cameron-tory-rebellion-europe (Accessed: 7th March 2020).

WELFENS, P. J. J. (2016). Cameron's information disaster in the referendum of 2016: an exit from Brexit? *International Economics and Economic Policy*, 13(4), pp.539-548.

WHITMAN, R.G. (2016a). The UK and EU Foreign, Security and Defence Policy after Brexit: Integrated, Associated or Detached? *National Institute Economic Review*, 238(1), pp. R43-R50.

WHITMAN, R.G. (2016b). The UK and the EU Foreign and Security Policy: An optional Extra. *The Political Quarterly*, 87(2), pp.254-261.

WINTOUR, P. (2014). 'Labour pledges to repeal Lobbying Act in transparency drive'. *The Guardian*. 3rd April. Available at: https://www.theguardian.com/politics/2014/apr/03/labour-pledge-repeal-lobbying-act-transparency (Accessed: 27th February 2020).

Definitions

'Referendum'. In Merriam-Webster's online dictionary: Definition of the word "REFERENDUM". Available at http:// https://www.merriam-webster.com/dictionary/referendum (Accessed: 3rd February 2020).

YOUR KNOWLEDGE HAS VALUE

- We will publish your bachelor's and
  master's thesis, essays and papers

- Your own eBook and book -
  sold worldwide in all relevant shops

- Earn money with each sale

Upload your text at www.GRIN.com
and publish for free